IN: Incarnation & Inclusion,
Abba & Lamb
Copyright © 2019 Bradley Jersak

All rights reserved. No portion of this book may be reproduced, stored in any form except for brief quotations in reviews or articles, without prior permission from the author.

Published by St. Macrina Press

Editorial services: Felicia Murrell
The Bee Company - www.yzcounsel.com

Bible Translations

NTE: Default New Testament references are from N.T. Wright, *The New Testament for Everyone* [also titled *The Kingdom New Testament: A Contemporary Translation*] (SPCK, 2011).

DBH: David Bentley Hart, *The New Testament: A Translation* (Yale, 2018).

HB: Default Old Testament references are from Robert Alter, The Hebrew Bible: A Translation with Commentary (Norton, 2019).

Emphases: All emphases throughout the book are the author's, including Scripture texts and cited material, unless indicated.

ISBN: 978-1-0824-6173-6

Jersak, Bradley Mark, 1964 —
IN: Incarnation & Inclusion, Abba & Lamb / Bradley Jersak
1. Nonfiction— Religion — Ecumenism & Interfaith

St. Macrina Press
Abbotsford, BC | www.bradjersak.com

Incarnation & Inclusion, Abba & Lamb

Bradley Jersak

for Peter and Anne-Marie Helms

Before I even knew you, you included me.
When others excluded me, you welcomed me.
Even when it cost you, you stood with me.
Like Jesus.
Prost!

CONTENTS

OVERTURE / Eden Jersak
switching trees / *9*

FULL DISCLOSURE
a preface / *13*

RADICAL UNIQUENESS
the Light, the Word, the Name & the Lamb / *19*

RADICAL INCLUSION
conflicting visions of righteousness / *41*

RADICAL INTIMACY
my *Abba* / *69*

RADICAL ENGAGEMENT
toddlers with crayons / *83*

RADICAL ENCOUNTERS
seven stories / *101*

RADICAL RELEASE
the priest at Jesus' feet / *125*

FINIS
in practice: a consummation / *157*

RESPONSE / Jamie & Donna Winship
in conversation: "kingdom circles" / *163*

APPENDIX I
five witnesses: a confirmation / *171*

APPENDIX II
important definitions:

inclusion, pluralism, syncretism / *179*

OVERTURE / Eden Jersak switching trees

BRAD AND I MET for the first time in September of 1982. We were just two of the hundreds of budding theologians at our chosen bible college. We were eighteen-years-old and enjoyed the surety of knowing who was "IN" and who was "OUT." I shudder now at the memory of our misguided prejudgments and the broad strokes of our condemnation of others.

My eyes were opened just a little bit in those years at college, surprised by the depth of faith and understanding I discovered in my co-eds who had grown up in other Christian denominations. Somewhere along the line, I had picked up the idea that everyone outside my church affiliation was a lesser Christian. If pushed, I may have even questioned Brad's Baptist upbringing as a bit shaky.

In our third year of college, we segued our friendship into dating and began to spend a lot more time together. I recall one discussion we had about divorce and remarriage, and how we thought being remarried would throw a person into a perpetual state of sin, which of course would ensure the person would be "OUT" on the Day of Judgment.

In those days and through the following decades, we would spend a lot of time figuring out, either quietly in our own minds or in heated discussions at the table, who was "IN" and

Overture: Eden Jersak

who was "OUT." What we hadn't realized is that we were sitting under "the Tree of The Knowledge of Good and Evil," gobbling the forbidden fruit and wasting our precious time sorting and judging what we could not possibly know!

I can't say exactly when the dawning began—gradual and very subtle shifts in our hearts provided new vantage points for us to discover. But slowly, we began to shift, to see God even in those who hadn't arrived, in those who couldn't even comprehend what God was offering.

Brad was a youth pastor for a decade, and we were witnesses of God's extravagant love for kids who were coming to youth with no history or understanding of God. Many even met Christ outside the youth group, because some of our teens were praying with kids at school and God would "show up," as we'd say in those days. Apparently, God wasn't nearly as picky about the rules of inclusion as we were.

Then in 1998, we planted a church and again discovered that God's arms were open much wider than we were aware. Our church was made up of people with disabilities, prodigals returning home, children, addicts in recovery or still battling their disease, the poor and the rest of us—the ones who thought we had it all together. It was chaos on a good Sunday and bedlam on the worst. But we began to see that whether our disabilities were evident or hidden, whether we were actual children or adult children, whether our addictions were manageable or out of control, and whether our bank book balanced or we couldn't even afford a bank book, God's image was stamped on each of us!

Our steps forward were painfully slow; our progress was incremental but our hearts always desired to be faithful and teachable. But even our inclusion was still cloistered in our church, focused on those who we deemed were at least trying. Our measurement of who was "IN" and who was "OUT" had enlarged marginally. The problem was that we still clung to our measuring stick, seeking shade under the Tree of the Knowledge of Good and Evil.

Personally, I think my most significant shift towards the Tree of Life happened when I began to recall what my mother modeled for us in my childhood. I remembered that no matter how difficult we were at the dinner table, we were never made to leave. We were expected to stay put in all our misery. We were never banished for our bad behavior or excluded because of something we had done.

My mom exemplified this further every time she invited the "black sheep" of the family to our family Christmas events. That was confusing to me as a child because in my mind and in our culture, they were most certainly "Out," yet that never deterred my mom from inviting them to our table.

Looking back, those are some of the clearest examples I've seen of God's heart toward his family. So often, we have chosen to believe that only the kids who behave, who follow the narrow path and say the magic prayer are IN the family. But the prodigal son was never less than a son. He just missed out on the benefits of the sonship that had always been his.

Now, thirty-three years into our marriage, we are feeling the freedom of not having to waste our time and energy sorting

Overture: Eden Jersak

people into our imaginary IN and OUT camps. We can lay under the Tree of Life and enjoy the fruit of life that fills us with the hope that God is far more loving and inclusive than our old measuring sticks could fathom.

Brad has demonstrated his willingness to stick his neck out on this account. I have seen him validate those who have been shut out by the church and discarded by Christians. He has repeatedly and with lovingkindness invited them to the table and valued them as God values them. When he writes, he recognizes that if he errs, he must err on the side of hope. This is not a theoretical book—it's a book of our experiences and discoveries of how wide and deep, long and high God's love is for each of us, for all of us.

Eden Jersak

FULL DISCLOSURE
a preface

"'DOES THAT MEAN,' said Mack, 'that all roads lead to you?'
'Not at all.' Jesus smiled as he reached for the door handle to the shop. 'Most roads don't lead anywhere. What it does mean is that I will travel any road to find you.'"
—Wm. Paul Young, *The Shack*

THE QUESTION:
Inclusive Gospel and Unique Savior

The question I address in this brief work is how Christ-followers might hold the tension of these two abiding and complementary truths:

1. Christ's one-of-a-kind revelation
2. Abba's all-inclusive love

I believe that sacred Scripture and Christ himself affirm both these doctrines in a mind-blowing fullness. And yet those who enthusiastically profess either one of these two truths frequently do so at the expense of their complement.

On one hand, exclusivists gravitate to such central texts as John 14:6 and Acts 4:12, where Christ is identified as the only way and the only name by whom the Father—the *Abba*

Full Disclosure

revealed in Jesus—may be known. Intrinsic to their interpretation of that claim may arise an exclusive us-them, in-out dualism in which explicit recognition of Christ's identity and right belief in his claims comprise the one and only narrow gateway of access to his *Abba*.

That begs some questions. Does this mean no one prior to Christ knew God? Does this mean God's love only extends to no one since then outside the Christian faith?

The flip side, nothing new but growing in momentum, is a broad pluralism that recognizes *Abba's* love as all-inclusive. This crowd sees all people within God's embrace and all faiths as equally valid (or equally redundant) paths to the Divine. In their reaction to exclusivism, pluralists and syncretists may reject any unique truth-claims about Christ to be intolerable. For more on inclusion, pluralism and syncretism (as I use the terms), see "Appendix II: Important Definitions."

In light of *Abba's* all-inclusive love, we're left wondering whether Christ himself is necessary, optional or dispensable. Many are moving on, finding Christianity (and even Christ) too constrictive for their universally inclusive vision.

APPROACH

I am neither an exclusivist nor a pluralist. I believe in both the unique revelation of Christ and the inclusive love of *Abba*. In the following study, I'll lay out biblical and experiential evidence for integrating and celebrating both these truths together, espousing the beautiful gospel of Christ's unique revelation of *Abba's* all-inclusive love.

By "Christ," I am not referring to some abstract, ethereal or disincarnate spirit. Following the Apostolic tradition, I mean specifically our "one Lord Jesus Christ," the Lamb crucified and risen, whose singular revelation unveiled God as our eternal, cruciform and loving *Abba*.

My primary lens for this synthesis is the prologue of John's Gospel, where I see:

God's One and Only Lamb, crucified and risen–
    this Word who speaks ALL into being,
    this Light who shines on *all* and in *all*,
    this Life who breathes life into *all*,
    this One unveils God as
        Our
          All-merciful,
        All-embracing
        ***Abba*.**

I, for one, believe that *God's banqueting table is wide open because of Christ. The higher my Christology, the wider I see the reach of Abba's love.* The banquet metaphor is a way to think about both the uniqueness of Christ and the inclusivity of his *Abba*. The Master of the feast instructed his servants to invite, nay, to *compel all* to join in the feast. There's a seat and setting reserved for every human in history. I hope this book magnifies both these glorious truths clearly.

My approach to the question will be to bring together biblical revelation, real-life anecdotes and authoritative witnesses in a three-fold interdependent testimony.

Full Disclosure

Thus, I intend to emulate Luke's method in the Book of Acts. One of his key agendas was to walk his readership into Peter and Paul's radical revelation of Gentile inclusion via Christ's new covenant.

To do that, Luke introduces Simon Peter as the premier apostle in the first phase of the early church. He systematically builds a case for Peter's authority. Simon is the presiding apostle at Pentecost and the church's primary spokesman. Luke follows his career, highlighting the signs and wonders of Peter's ministry: supernatural prison breaks, miraculous healings (including a resurrection) and even the baffling incident of Ananias and Sapphira's demise at his feet.

All of this sets us up for Peter's vision of the sheet full of unclean things descending from heaven. This prepares both him and us for his encounter with the Gentile general Cornelius. Cornelius' conversion will ultimately converge with Paul's epiphany on the Road to Damascus as the two storylines intersect at the first Council of Jerusalem. There, James, the brother of Jesus leads the Christian motherhouse as they weave together Scripture, testimony and apostolic authority to recognize how Christ's unique revelation opens up *Abba's* universal love to all nations.

The process is not limited to a theological prescription rooted in biblical exegesis and then applied to our situation—as in the standard modernist approach. Rather, as is often the case in Scripture and especially in the Gospels and Acts, our theology refracts and reflects our experience—an encounter with the living God. Only in that relationship do we find the people of God gathering in theological reflection of these strange new events.

This book, though certainly rooted in my own biblical and theological studies, mimics the apostles' commitment to evaluating real-life events, especially among those who, like Cornelius, apparently knew God prior to Christian faith and then found Christ taking them into a deeper experience of *Abba's* love.

For the eyewitnesses of Christ and the church in Acts, their experience generated a fresh investigation of the Scriptures and the theological analyses that followed.

As best I can tell, both Cornelius and the friends I describe herein first encountered God as the Light and the Word (Christ incognito). Then later, Christ unveiled himself to them overtly—sometimes directly, sometimes through a witness. Once they meet Christ, he leads them into the revelation of intimate communion with his *Abba*.

That's the path and phenomenon I'll be examining through stories and Scriptures. I believe that *Abba's* love revealed in Christ is radically inclusive. In my view, *Abba's* inclusion and embrace are established in and inseparable from Christ's radical uniqueness. In Christ, we experience *Abba's* universal love and cosmic reconciliation.

Before addressing each aspect of this indivisible pairing, here is the whole picture in brief:

- God is known through Christ—the Light, the Life and the Word of all-merciful Love. That's my own bottom line and life message.

Full Disclosure

- The God revealed and experienced uniquely in the Incarnation of Christ is his *Abba* and ours.
- While every human being bears the image of God, we see the fullness and perfection of *Abba's* mirror image in the face of Jesus Christ. While great prophets across spiritual traditions have endeavored to faithfully direct us toward God, Christ alone said, "If you've seen me, you've seen my *Abba.*"
- The *Abba* revealed through the life of Christ is radically inclusive love, indiscriminately gracious and kind, open and accessible to all, and utterly responsive to every groping impulse for divine mercy, however religious or irreligious.
- Religious labels such as pluralism, syncretism or exclusivism (none of which I hold) all relate to humanity's awkward, flailing pursuit of God. They don't interest me or apply to this project. Rather, the uniqueness of Christ is *Abba's* gracious pursuit of us despite our best and worst efforts, even at the risk of seeming to endorse them in his condescension to meet us as we are.

Having laid out the connection between the *Abba* of inclusion and his "only begotten" or "one and only Son," we can now examine each facet individually.

RADICAL UNIQUENESS
the Light, the Word, the Name & the Lamb

UNIQUENESS & INCLUSION

HOLDING THE UNIQUE REVELATION OF CHRIST and the inclusive love of our *Abba* together has never been easy for Christians. We forever corner ourselves into sounding either too broad or too narrow. But in the back of our minds and hearts is an authentic desire to be faithful to the wideness of *Abba's* mercy *and* the singularity of Christ's Person and work.

How do we hold both?

Back to the Beginning—as seen from the end. And so I find myself in the wondrous Prologue of John's Gospel. We call him St. John the Theologian. Why? Because he names God.

JOHN'S COSMIC INCARNATION

Let's return to the Scriptures. In the Nativity accounts of Matthew, Mark and Luke, we meet the Virgin, the shepherds, the wise men, the angels and 8 lb. 6 oz. baby Jesus. In contrast, John's "Prologue" (John 1:1-18) retells the Incarnation story on a cosmic scale. We might call it "John's cosmic Incarnation," remembering it encompasses far more than the Nativity narrative. Here is his account, highlighting keys words:

Radical Uniqueness

In the beginning was the **Word**. The **Word** was with God, and the **Word** was God. The **Word** was with God in the beginning.

All things came into existence through him; not one thing that exists came into existence without him. Life was in him, and this life was the **Light** of the human race. The **Light** shines in the darkness, and the darkness did not overcome it.

There was a man called John, who was sent from God. He came as evidence, to be a witness for the **Light**, so that everyone might believe through him. He was not himself the **Light**, but he came to give evidence about the **Light**.

The true **Light**, which gives **light** to every human being, was coming into the world. He was in the world, and the world was made through him, and the world did not know him.

He came to what was his own, and his own people did not accept him. But to anyone who did accept him, he gave the right to be called God's children; yes, to anyone who believed in his name.

They were not born from blood, or from fleshly desire, or from the intention of a man, but from God.

And the **Word** became flesh and lived among us. We gazed upon his glory, glory like that of the *Abba's* only Son, full of grace and truth.

John [the Baptist] was a witness for him, loud and clear.

> "This is the one," he said, "that I was speaking about when I told you, 'The one who comes after me ranks ahead of me, because he was before me.'"
>
> Yes, it's out of his fullness that we have all received, grace indeed on top of grace. The law, you see, was given through Moses; grace and truth came through **Jesus Christ**. Nobody has ever seen God. The only-begotten God, who is intimately close to the *Abba*—he has brought him to **light**.

So far, John has identified the **Word** and the **Light** with God and as God. He has also said this Word became flesh and his name is **Jesus Christ**, the *only begotten God* who alone reveals God as *Abba*. But there is another layer in verses 29-34.

> The next day [John the Baptist] saw Jesus coming toward him and declared, *"Here is the **Lamb of God** who takes away the sin of the world!* This is he of whom I said, 'After me comes a man who ranks ahead of me because he was before me.' I myself did not know him; but I came baptizing with water for this reason, that he might be revealed to Israel."
>
> And John testified, "I saw the Spirit descending from heaven like a dove, and it remained on him. I myself did not know him, but the one who sent me to baptize with water said to me, 'He on whom you see the Spirit descend and remain is the one who baptizes with the Holy Spirit.' And I myself have seen and have testified that this is the **Son of God**."

Radical Uniqueness

This paragraph is so critical because it not only associates the eternal **Word** and divine **Light** with the **Name** of Jesus Christ—John also anticipates the Passion of Christ upfront. "Behold, the ***Lamb***."

The same **Word** who was from the beginning, by whom all things were made, the same cosmic **Light** who said, "Let there be light" and shines his light on all, God's only begotten **Son** who unveils God as our *Abba—this One is the **Lamb***, crucified and risen, who takes away the sin of the world. This cruciform Lamb is the **Image** of *Abba's* kenotic nature and self-giving Love. This **Lamb**, slain from the foundation of the world, is the One in whose **Image** humanity was formed!

HIGH POINTS

Let's now review the high points of John's Prologue:

The Light

- The **Light** is the **light** of the human race, not just Christians.
- The **Light** shone in the darkness, not just in the bright places.
- The **Light** has a witness who points to the **Light**—John in this case.
- Some believe in the **Light** and welcome that **Light**.
- Others reject the **Light** but cannot overcome it.
- The **Light** became evident in this world.
- The **Light** is true and the true **Light** gives light to everyone.

Note on verse 9: whether "coming into the world" refers to

IN: INCARNATION & INCLUSION

Christ or to the people, either translation holds that the Light shines universally—on everyone, not just Christians.

The Word

- The **Word** was "in the beginning."
- The **Word** was with God.
- The **Word** was God.
- From the **Word** came the entire cosmos.
- From the **Word** came all *Life*.
- The **Word** became *Flesh*.
- The **Word** revealed *Abba*.

The Name

- The **Light** that shines has a **Name**.
- The **Word** that speaks has a **Name**.
- By this **Name** we know God as ***Abba***.
- By this **Name** we are saved.
- The **Name** of the **Word** and the **Name** of the **Light** is **Jesus Christ**.

Name here designates the *Person*, their identity and nature; it's not just their moniker. That's an imperative distinction, as we'll see, since we may know the Person by various names *or* imposters may steal the Name and commit identity theft.

The Lamb

- The **Lamb** has appeared in space-time history.
- The **Lamb** designates the **Word** enfleshed, crucified under Pontius Pilate, buried and resurrected.
- The **Lamb** takes away the sin of the world.

Radical Uniqueness

Note that the **Lamb** does not merely *offer* to take away the sin of the world. The Lamb does not merely take away the sin of the church or the elect or the righteous. And the Lamb does not merely take away the *sin(s)* of the world—"sin" (singular) indicates something more fundamental has been dealt with. Sin is the disease of disunion healed in the Lamb's union with humanity, *all* humanity.

Cosmic Thoughts

- The **Light**, the **Word** and the **Name** (Person) are One and the same.
- The **Light** shines on everyone.
- The **Word** speaks to anyone.
- The **Name** is Jesus Christ.
- The **Name** awaits a witness.
- The witness points to the **Lamb**, Christ crucified and risen, who takes away the sin of the *world*.
- The **Lamb** is the perfect Image of true deity and the *telos* of true humanity.

Persistent Questions

The highlights I've selected provoke some persistent questions, at least in me:

If Christ is the **Name** of the **Light** that shines on everyone, and if Christ is the **Word** of God who speaks to anyone, and if Christ is the **Lamb** who has taken away the sin of the world,

- Can you know the **Light** and follow the **Word** prior to or possibly without ever knowing the **Name** (the Person) is Jesus Christ?

IN: INCARNATION & INCLUSION

- Didn't Abraham know God? Didn't Moses? Didn't David? Didn't Elijah and Isaiah?
- What about Acts 4:12? "Rescue won't come from anybody else! There is *no other **name*** given under heaven and among humans by which we must be rescued."
- But now Jesus has come. Did knowing the **Name** only become necessary then? Is Christ's arrival bad news for those who don't know the **Name**? Are they now doomed until they do?
- If they aren't doomed, what advantage is there to knowing the **Name**?
- Did the Lamb in fact take away the sin of the world? What if we don't know that? Is knowing it necessary for it to be true? What difference does it make? What is the benefit of knowing?

CALLING ON THE NAME OF THE LORD

Given Christ's relentless love for all humanity and his superabundant competence as a truly Good Shepherd and given the breadth and variety of human spiritual experiences, consider the following problem. I grew up with the following Evangelical syllogism drawn from Romans 10:

1. Only those who confess Jesus as Lord are IN:

> If you confess with your mouth that Jesus is Lord and believe in your heart that God raised him from the dead, you shall be saved.
>
> —Romans 10:9

Radical Uniqueness

2. Only those who call on the Name of the Lord will be IN:

"Everyone who calls on the Name of the Lord will be saved." How then can they call on the One in whom they have not believed? *And how can they believe in the One of whom they have not heard?* And how can they hear without someone to preach? And how can they preach unless they are sent? As it is written: "How beautiful are the feet of those who bring good news!"
—Romans 10:13-15

3. Only those who hear the Name of the Lord and believe it will be IN:

For Isaiah says, "Lord, who has *believed* our message?" Consequently, *faith comes from hearing the message,* and the message is heard through the word about Christ.
—Romans 10:17

Is Paul saying that only those who hear the gospel of Jesus Christ, believe it by faith and confess it as their own can know God and be "saved"? It sure sounds like it.

That's what I was taught. I myself taught it. That sounds like what Paul is saying, right? We may read it that way IF we strain the passage through the filter of Christian exclusivism and totalize it for all people in every era—and so we have. We've often interpreted Romans 10 to say you can only know God and "get in" by confession of Christian faith. And it makes sense ... IF Paul's words are snatched from their context.

But in fact, the whole context of Romans 9-11 outlines Paul's hope that even his Jewish family who've so far rejected

IN: INCARNATION & INCLUSION

Christ will ultimately *all* be "saved"—ALL of them. Here is the answer to his heart-cry and punchline to his argument:

> That is how *'all Israel shall be saved,'* as the Bible says:
> The Deliverer will come from Zion,
> and will turn away ungodliness from Jacob.
> —Romans 11:26

Further, we read that "God has not left himself without a witness" (Acts 14:17). Some extrapolate from Romans 2:12-16 that everyone knows enough about God (through nature and conscience) to be damned—but they can only be redeemed by hearing and responding to our gospel. Without hearing the good news and until they do, they are "unreached" and therefore "unsaved" and therefore "damned."

But consider how this thoroughly "biblical" (i.e., proof-texted) logic makes God less than the relentless and competent Shepherd revealed in Christ.

SECOND ATTEMPT

What if God's logic is far broader and more gracious than we assumed. What if we read Paul this way?

1. God never leaves himself without a witness:

> The common Grace of the Holy Spirit ensures that *anyone*, anywhere, at any time, can find God. In Paul's address to the Athenians (Acts 17), he says God isn't far from any of us. He says we are *all* God's offspring. He says we *all* swim in God's presence, even when we're still praying to the "unknown God."

Radical Uniqueness

2. Everyone (Jew or Gentile), anywhere, anytime who calls on the name of the Lord will be saved (cf. Acts 2:21):

> And while God has *many names* in the Bible—Christ himself assures us that anyone who seeks God and asks for God's help will find it (Matt. 7:7-8). Jesus promises that *Abba* will hear and answer. Why? Because God is a Good Shepherd, already seeking all of us.

3. Finally, God has revealed himself through Christ:

> Just as God had previously been known through the testimony of nature, the living prophets and the written Scriptures, so now the zenith of Abba's self-revelation has arrived in Jesus. Paul says, "we believe in one God, *Abba,* and one Lord, Jesus Christ" (1 Cor. 8:6).

Paul wants his Jewish kinsmen, his Gentile audience (and all of us) to know that when we call on the Lord, we are calling on *Abba* through Jesus Christ our Lord.

And whenever Moses, for example, encountered God, his experience of *Abba* was through Christ. At least this is how the author of Hebrews saw it:

"By faith Moses ... regarded disgrace *for the sake of Christ* as of greater value than the treasures of Egypt, because he was looking ahead to his reward" (Heb. 11:24, 26).

BY ANY NAME?

Here's the $64,000 question: does Paul believe that anyone who sincerely prays to God by any moniker is in reality calling on *Abba* through Jesus Christ? Even before they know his true identity? Even addicts who seek help from a nameless

IN: INCARNATION & INCLUSION

"higher power?" Or are they just worshiping idols?

Back to Athens, remember Paul's message to the "religious pagans" there?

> So Paul stood up in the midst of the Areopagus.
>
> "Men of Athens," he said, "I see that you are in every way an extremely religious people. For as I was going along and looking at your objects of worship, I saw an altar with the inscription, TO AN UNKNOWN GOD.
>
> Well, I'm here to tell you about *what it is that you are worshipping in ignorance*. The God who made the world and everything in it, the one who is Lord of heaven and earth, doesn't live in temples made by human hands. Nor does he need to be looked after by human hands, as though he lacked something, since he himself gives life and breath and all things to everyone. He made from one stock every race of humans to live on the whole face of the earth, allotting them their properly ordained times and the boundaries for their dwellings.
>
> The aim was that they would search for God, and perhaps reach out for him and find him. Indeed, he is actually not far from each one of us, for in him we live and move and exist; as also some of your own poets have put it, 'For we are his offspring.'"
>
> —Acts 17:22-28

For Paul, regardless of the **name** (moniker) we use and even in our ignorance of the **Name** (identity of the Person), for those who sincerely pray for God's help, there is only one God who is actually there, only one God who can hear and only

Radical Uniqueness

one God who ever answers. Whatever moniker we use, Jesus Christ is the Way to *Abba* and the Image of *Abba,* so argues Paul to the Athenians, even while stepping up as a witness to the **Name**.

True, our understanding of God may be idolatrous, to the degree that the image we conceive is unChristlike. This is as true for Christians as it is for any other worshipers. On the other hand, despite our ignorance, *Abba* patiently walks us out of idolatry toward his true and Christlike Image.

After interacting with twelve-step recovery fellowships for ten years, I can bear witness that the program takes addicts on a journey from broken and idolatrous misunderstandings of their higher power to the God who is loving, caring and forgiving—i.e., Christlike. I wish to God our churches all had that same track record.

My point is that many addicts had experienced the liberating **Light** of Christ long before they recognized his **Name**. How? Through the **Grace** of the Holy Spirit.

Now we're saying something both radically inclusive and exclusive at once.

I'd better be more specific:

LER, LORD O' THE SEA

Let's pretend I'm an Irish fisher living in the ninth century. I own a little boat and often find myself in waves big enough to capsize me. According to the tradition of my people, I pray to Ler—god of the sea in Irish mythology. Everyone does in our wee fishing village. I'm a good man who loves my family and labors hard to put food on our table. We are always grate-

IN: INCARNATION & INCLUSION

ful for the fish that Ler provides—we find him to be generous and always thank Ler when we have enough stores to get through the winter. Ler was good to us this year—we even had enough to share with others who need help—such as the widow Abigail down the lane.

One day, I'm a good distance out at sea and a storm catches me off guard. The boy—wee Sean—and I are bailing water as fast as we can but it's no use. The waves eventually take us into a stony bar, and the boat is shattered to a thousand splinters. I'm able to grab a plank for flotation but I can't see Sean. My wife'll kill me if I lose him. I cry out for him, "Sean! Where are ya, lad?!" No answer. I dive beneath the waves to look—too murky. Panic is strangling me and I can barely keep my own nose above the salty sea.

"Ler!" I cry. "Ler, help us!"

Nothing.

Again, "Ler, Lord o' the sea, save us!"

Suddenly, I see a swath of wet and bloodied hair float by and I grab my son. I pull him to me and despite my exhaustion, Ler graciously throws us onto a sandbar. We are saved!

Quiz

1. Does Ler exist? No. There is no Ler. Ler is a mythological made-up god.
2. Did Ler hear me and save us? No. Ler has no ears, cannot hear and does not save. Ler doesn't exist.
3. But I prayed and was miraculously saved. I was desperately praying. Did anyone hear? Did anyone answer? Did anyone save?

Radical Uniqueness

4. Does *Abba* hear and answer the desperate cries of those who don't yet know his Name? What is more important to God? Hearing the correct moniker or hearing our hearts and answering our prayers?

Answer Key

Exodus 2-3–Israel didn't know the name YHWH, yet he heard and answered their cries.

PATRIARCH BARTHOLOMEW

According to Patriarch Bartholomew, "We are all created by God and as such we are all brothers and sisters. We have the same heavenly Father, *whatever we call him.*"

In a TV interview, the Patriarch's host pressed this question, "All religions have the same heavenly Father?"

Bartholomew replied, "Of course. God is but one, independently of the **name** we give him, Allah or Yahweh, and so on. God is one and we are his children." (Charlie Rose Interview, Nov. 2, 2009).

Really? Isn't this the slippery path of pluralism? All paths lead to God and all religions are equally valid?

You might hear that, but his Eminence didn't say that at all. His claims are really quite conservative, biblical and modest. Let's review them by quizzing ourselves. How would our answers stack up to his:

- He claims there is only one God. Do you?
- He claims that there is only one Creator. Do you?

IN: INCARNATION & INCLUSION

- He claims this one Creator fathered all humanity. That there is only one heavenly Father. Do you?
- He claims that our limited, conflicting religious beliefs and various monikers do not negate points 1-3. Do you? If not, which point is no longer valid?

I don't hear Bartholomew claiming more than that. I don't hear him validating all religious paths as equal, valid or true. He is simply affirming "one God, the Father Almighty, Creator of heaven and earth, and of all things visible and invisible."

Would you? I would.

Is there more to say? Of course there is. Read on!

What about Jesus? If I don't know God's moniker or use the wrong name, yet *Abba* still graciously answers, does that mean knowing the **Name** (Person) of Jesus doesn't matter? We're back to that question again.

The answer is that Jesus' **Name** does matter. Enormously. So, please read on.

JOHN WESLEY–"ON FAITH"

The issues around *Abba's* inclusive love and Christ's unique revelation aren't new questions. Christ-followers from earliest times asked them with all sincerity.

John Wesley (the eighteenth-century evangelist), thought through them carefully, particularly because he sought to bring the name of Jesus Christ to North America's indigenous people. Many he met seemed to already know the Creator prior to hearing the gospel—which begs the question, why evangelize?

Radical Uniqueness

I'm going to frame his questions and responses in the form of my own direct interview, drawing from an article he wrote "On Faith":

Brad: John Wesley, your experiences as an evangelist and missionary raise two important questions as I ponder *Abba's* inclusive love and Christ's singular revelation.

First, from your point of view, what if someone—a First Nations chief you've met, for example—has obviously turned to the **Light** and followed the **Word** but still doesn't know the **Name**?

Wesley: A divine conviction of God, and the things of God, even in its infant state, enables everyone that possesses it to fear God and work righteousness. Whosoever, in every nation, believes thus far, the Apostle declares is accepted.

Brad: Your manner of speech is peculiar.

Wesley: Look who's talking.

Brad: Okay, if I hear you right, when they turn to the **Light** with conviction and devotion, and when they follow the **Word** in their worship and their walk, God sees their faith as acceptable.

Wesley: Yes. This is the testimony of the apostle Peter concerning Cornelius.

Brad: I get that. But I also notice that God didn't stop there. Having accepted Cornelius, declaring his life righteous and his heart clean, God still sends him to Peter to hear the gospel of Jesus. To bear witness to the **Name**.

So, my second question is, what advantage do you see in sharing the **Name** to people who've already turned to the

Light and followed the **Word**? It's the same Person, right? Some people even believe that sharing the **Name** endangers those people of rejecting the **Light**!

Wesley: Only if those bringing the **Name** are boors and buffoons. Perhaps the question itself belies a craven poltroon? Please excuse my foul and unfamiliar tongue.

Brad: Believe me—I get it. But what then is the advantage of sharing the **Name** of Jesus with those already accepted by God?

Wesley: The advantage, young man, is two-fold:

1. In knowing the Name, *we enjoy the full benefits of the redeemed life.*

In the **Name** of Christ, we come to know God as Father, not as servants but as dear sons and daughters. In Acts 10, when Cornelius (a God-fearing pagan) heard Peter's gospel, he came into his inheritance in the Father's house. Though he had known God previously, he now received the Holy Spirit who reveals God as *Abba* and Christ as Lord. Cornelius had not known this intimacy even as a generous, prayerful God-fearer. The gospel baptized him in the fire of divine Love.

2. Second, in knowing the Name, *we enjoy the full assurance of our salvation* **based on what Christ has done.**

This assurance comes not from the sincerity of our prayers nor by the righteousness of our deeds. Our confidence is in the faithfulness of Christ, whose gospel reveals God's mercy, secures our salvation and guarantees our resurrection. Hearing this gospel, Cornelius experienced the greater riches of eternal life: communion with Father, Son and Holy Spirit.

Radical Uniqueness

Brad: Thus, rightly shared in word and deed, the **Name** of Christ and his gospel cause the **Light** of Christ to blaze even more brightly in our hearts and the **Word** of Christ to resound more clearly in our minds. Hearing the **Name** of the **Light** and the **Word** should be cause for great rejoicing!

Wesley: Don't try to sound like me. You're not good at it. But yes. Therefore, I watch carefully for the **Light** they have and share boldly the **Name** we have.

OUR MARVELOUS INHERITANCE

If Wesley was correct, and I believe he was, then through his Incarnation, Christ reconciled us to *Abba,* he united and reunited humanity and Trinity in his Person. On the Cross, Christ tore open the curtain for *all Abba's* children, granting everyone, everywhere complete access to *Abba's* house now and forevermore.

That's our inheritance.

But who is "our"? Only Christians, right?

That's not what we've heard from Paul.

Here's Paul: As in Adam, Paradise was lost for all; so in Christ, Paradise is reopened for all.

But not everyone knows this.

Exactly. That's why John Wesley became an evangelist!

That's the astounding Good News that Christ commissioned his apostles to share! That's the feast to which his servants invite and compel everyone to attend. The message is, "You're included! You're IN! So please, come on IN!"

St. Hilary of Poitiers was a fourth-century evangelist. If we

IN: INCARNATION & INCLUSION

were to tell him, "Everyone's included, so let's dispense with all this embarrassing Jesus-talk," he would be dumbfounded.

"What?" he might gasp. "And fail to share the inheritance?" He'd regard us as greedy hoarders who refused to notify the rest of the family they'd been named in Christ's extravagant living will!

I can see him now, in the communion of saints, opening the Scriptures to expound on the inheritance secured through the Cross (i.e., the death and resurrection) of Christ:

> Every action, therefore, and performance of miracles by Christ are most great and divine and marvelous: but the most marvelous of all is his precious Cross. For no other thing has subdued death, expiated the sin of the first parent, despoiled Hades, bestowed the resurrection, granted the power to us of contemning [scorning] the present and even death itself, prepared the return to our former blessedness, opened the gates of Paradise, given our nature a seat at the right hand of God, and made us the children and heirs of God, save the Cross of our Lord Jesus Christ. For by the Cross all things have been made right.
>
> —Hilary of Poitiers, "Concerning the Cross and here further concerning Faith"

He'd be like, "Exactly what part of that inheritance did you think was not worth sharing? Haven't you experienced it yourself? Or don't you believe in him?"

For Hilary, as for Wesley, it's not that signing off on the

Radical Uniqueness

inheritance in our baptism earns it for anyone. Indeed, many are already obviously drawing from it! Rather, many are not yet aware of the fullness of their inheritance and have yet to begin enjoying it. The role of the "Royal Priesthood" is to deliver the beautiful news of such great wealth to *all*.

THERE'S MORE: A FAMILY

In a discussion with a group of friends in Ontario, I was describing John Wesley's convictions about our assurance and our inheritance in Christ.

To these benefits, Rebecca added this happy insight:

> I like that you're alluding to the inheritance because I picture it like my dad who's doing this ancestry.com thing. We keep linking to our family back in Scotland and it's like that moment where you're finding your family too. Like you've turned toward the **Light** and then you find all these other people.
>
> "Hey, we belong together and these are my people and this is my actual inheritance and it stretches all the way back through history." It's beautiful!

THE FULLNESS OF HUMANITY: DIVINIZATION

As I reviewed Wesley's case with my mentor Ron Dart, he reminded me of a fourth aspect of our Christian inheritance: "deification" (also known as "divinization" or "theosis").

What is included in the *fullness* of our inheritance? Exclusive to the Christian vision is our doctrine of the deification of humanity, which exceeds even the strongest claims of Judaism or Islam. Human nature divinized is part of our inheritance through participation in the divine nature.

When you weaken your Christology, you weaken humanity by depriving it of divinization. This was Athanasius' case against Arius. The lower one's Christology, the lower the journey of humanity into its teleology into the divine nature.

What I hear Ron saying is that the Great Tradition of the early church saw Christ as the prototype of the new and true humanity. *Human destiny is to become divine by grace as Christ is by nature.* The original humanism of the Patristics (and its grand resurgence through Erasmus) saw far beyond the techno-evolution of Yuval Noah Harari's materialist *Homo Deus.* We will be transformed into much more than data and algorithms!

Our anthropology is rooted in and as expansive as our Christology. Only if Christ is alive and divine can we follow his Way through resurrection to our divinity. That aspect of our inheritance was neglected in Western Christianity, but it was there from the beginning (2 Cor. 3:18, 2 Pet. 1:4) and worthy of an entire book or two. I recommend Rowan Williams' *Being Human* and John Behr's *Becoming Human.*

THOUGHTS

1. We opened this chapter by acknowledging how difficult it can be to hold together *Abba's* all-inclusive love and Christ's

Radical Uniqueness

singular revelation. Has that been your experience? To which side does your faith tradition tilt? Where do you personally lean? Has this changed over time? What contributed to those changes?

2. John's "Prologue" describe Christ in cosmic terms— as the **Light** and the Logos (**Word**) who created the universe, sustains and pervades all places and times, and whose **Light** shines on *everyone*. Have you been a witness to this **Light** in your life? In your faith community? Beyond your faith community? Are you aware of those on whom, in whom or through whom the **Light** has shone brightly, even before they embraced the **Name** of the **Lamb**? Reflect on a particular instance with wonder and gratitude.

3. *Abba's* love has always been all-inclusive. How did the Incarnation reveal that? How did the life and teachings of Christ demonstrate it? How did the Cross (death and resurrection together) uniquely reveal *Abba's* all-inclusive love? What aspects of the gospel inheritance do you appreciate most? Hunger for most? Experience and enjoy most?

PRAYERS

Abba, thank you that your love reaches higher, wider, deeper and longer than I could ever imagine. Thank you for the Light, the Word and the Name that reopened Paradise and welcomed me in! Thank you that even in our ignorance of your Name or your true Image, you've made yourself known to all who call on you. Deepen in me the magnitude of our inheritance and the grace to share it freely.

RADICAL INCLUSION
conflicting visions
of righteousness

RADICAL INCLUSION

THE NEW JERUSALEM VISIONS of both Isaiah and John the Revelator are symbolic treasuries of Christ's radical inclusion (cf. Isa. 2:2-5, 25:6-9; 35:1-10 and Rev. 21-22). There, we see the River of Life that flows out of God's temple to *all* nations, along with the invitation of the Spirit and the Bride who say,

> "Come! Come to the waters! Let the kings of the earth bring the glory of the nations into the Temple! Come, drink of these waters. ALL are welcome. The gates of the city will never be shut!"

The River of Life is none other than our Lord Jesus Christ— the Fountain of Living Water whose love is poured out to *all* peoples. Christ welcomes and includes *all* who are thirsty, "Come! Drink deeply of my love!"

These visions are not deferred rewards for the faithful. They represent Christ's "Year of Jubilee" announcement (Lk. 4:8-21): "*Today*, these visions are fulfilled. *Today*, salvation is yours. *Today*, through me, you are in. You are *IN!*"

This triggered a question in the congregation: *"Them? THEY are in, too? The sick and the Sidonians and the Syrians?"*

Radical Inclusion

That didn't jive with the self-identifying insiders. Their idea of righteousness didn't include the substandard *them*. They go from zero to one hundred immediately, quick to make their first attempt on Christ's life.

"THEM? . . . Are you sure?"

We ask, you see, because even if we're not prone to violence, nearly everyone operates from a desire to be faithful—to be reckoned righteous before God. And our go to litmus test for faithfulness is often measured by in-out, us-them religious and ideological algorithms.

We ask, *"Even them?"* because God's people have long held conflicting visions of righteousness—historically and even biblically.

CONFLICTING VISIONS

Violent Zeal: Eradication

The Levites: In the Torah, two pivotal events establish violent zeal as markers of righteousness. First, you might recall the debacle of the golden calf (Exod. 32). Moses had ascended Mount Sinai to receive God's laws inscribed on stone tablets. He arrives back at camp with the good news, only to find the people dancing around a statue of gold.

> Moses' wrath flared, and he flung the tablets from his hand and smashed them at the bottom of the mountain. And he took the calf that they had made and burned it in fire and ground it fine and scattered it over water and made the Israelites drink it . . . And

IN: INCARNATION & INCLUSION

> Moses stood at the gate of the camp and said, "Whoever is for the LORD, to me!" And the Levites gathered round him. And he said to them, "Thus said the LORD God of Israel, 'Put every man his sword on his thigh, and cross over and back from gate to gate in the camp, and each man kill his brother and each man his fellow and each man his kin.'" And the Levites did according to the word of Moses, and about three thousand men of the people fell on the day. And Moses said, "Dedicate yourselves today to the LORD, for each man is against his son and against his brother, and so blessing may be given to you today."
> —Exodus 32:19-21, 26-29

Because they did not worship the golden calf and for their zealous, violent stand with Moses—slaughtering 3000 of their kinsmen—the Levites were permanently bequeathed the mantle of holy service to God in his tabernacle and temple (cf. Num. 32). This is God's "revolutionary guard."

> "For wholly given they [the Levites] are to me from the midst of the Israelites, instead of the breach of every womb, firstborn of all the Israelites . . . I consecrated them to me.
> —Numbers 8:16-17

Phinehas: Later, a specific Levite will distinguish himself righteous through another act of violent zeal. As the story goes, the people of Israel had won a series of wilderness battles with the Canaanite and Amorite tribes. The Moabites were

Radical Inclusion

terrified, so King Balak of Moab attempted to hire Balaam—a mercenary prophet adept at hexing nations. After several comical failed attempts in which he unwillingly blesses Israel with some beautiful prophecies (Num. 23-24), Balaam changes tactics and counsels King Balak, "*Include* [uh oh!] some Moabite women into the camp. Insert them into Israel's camp to seduce the men to bring the whole thing down."

Balaam's strategy worked perfectly: Before long, Israelite men were openly "whoring" with the Moabite women and worshiping their gods, including Baal Peor. Again, the wrath of God flared (apparently through Moses) saying, "Take all the chiefs of the people and impale them to the LORD before the sun, that the LORD's flaring wrath may turn away from Israel." This incredible disaster—resulting in a scourge of 24,000 people—climaxes when Phineas (Aaron's grandson) sees an Israelite with a Midianite woman and runs both of them through with a spear.

> And the LORD spoke to Moses, saying, "Phineas son of Eleazar son of Aaron the priest turned away My wrath from the Israelites when he zealously acted for My zeal in their midst, and I did not put an end to the Israelites through my zeal. Therefore say: I hereby grant him My covenant of peace. And it shall be for him and for his seed after him a covenant of perpetual priesthood in recompense for his acting zealously for his God and atoning for the Israelites."
> —Numbers 25:10-13

For his violent zeal on God's behalf, the Bible says, "And it was reckoned to him as righteousness" (Ps. 106:30)—the same language used for Abraham's faith! That's right: violent zeal was a vision of righteousness to solve *the problem of inclusion*.

Codified Zeal: Exclusion

Now, Israel was not meant to express their righteousness through endless cycles of sin and idolatry alternating with violent zeal. Rather, under the Levites, eradication is codified into Jewish Law as exclusion and expulsion.

If they didn't want a repeat of the golden calf and Phineas incidents again—if they hoped to avoid further blood purges—it made sense for Moses and his Levite posse to embed God's apparent desires into the legal code. One way to do that was to identify who was excluded.

We find all sorts of exclusion recorded in the Laws of Deuteronomy. Essentially, the Law says, "If you want it to go well with you, here is who is *OUT*." Law after law after law.

One of the laws that intrigues me is in Deuteronomy 23, where it says, "Now listen carefully. Here's who is *OUT*."

> A man shall not wed his father's wife, and shall not uncover his father's skirt. No one with crushed testes or a lopped member shall come into the LORD's assembly. No misbegotten shall come into the LORD's assembly. Even his tenth generation shall not come into the LORD's assembly. No Ammonite nor Moabite shall come into the LORD's assembly. Even his tenth generation shall not come into the LORD's assembly ever. Because they did not greet you with bread and

Radical Inclusion

> water on the way when you came out of Egypt, and for hiring against you Balaam son of Beor to curse you.
> —Deuteronomy 23:1-5

Wow. Let's review those rules:

First, if you've been emasculated through cutting or crushing, you're out! Lord, have mercy! Some translations specify the body parts. If you've become a eunuch or in some way castrated, voluntary or not, you are excluded.

Also, if you are "misbegotten"—born out of a forbidden or mixed marriage. Some translations say it's the child of a prostitute. Or some might assume this is a child born out of wedlock (think of Christ and his Torah-rigid opponents! See Jn. 8:41). But the clearest sense seems to be children of "forbidden marriage"—intermarriage to someone of another race or faith. And not only is that child *out*, so are their children, their grandchildren, their great-grandchildren—up to ten generations! An entire clan and tribe excluded. If you are the fruit of a forbidden marriage, you're out and you can't come in—*ever*.

And while we're at it, if you were an Ammonite or a Moabite, you're *out* too. You're not welcome. Why not? Because your ancestors didn't welcome the Israelites with water when they came out of Egypt, no matter how many centuries previous.

These exclusions multiply and become codified—codified as *exclusion, expulsion* and when necessary, *eradication*. Whether it's outsiders who bring their sin in or insiders having their sin float up, the solution is *exclusion*.

Enforced by the Levites: Notice that these laws of exclusion center around "the assembly"—the tabernacle in those days and later, the temple in Jerusalem. According to Deuteronomy 18, the Levites will be responsible for offenses connected to the temple. Their job is to identify offenders—to keep them out, to kick them out and when the Law says so, to arrest and punish wrongdoers.

That is to say, the Levites—the righteous agents of violent zeal and legal expulsion—become "the Temple Guard." As early as John 7, the chief priests and Pharisees send officers of the Temple Guard to arrest Jesus. Later, they will conspire with Judas to betray Jesus (Lk. 22:4). And yes, it is the Levite Temple Guard who arrest Jesus in Gethsemane (Lk. 22:52). Imagine!

In the name of "righteousness," they betray the Son of Righteousness himself! "Just following orders."

The New Covenant: a Subversive Righteousness

Above, I referred to conflicting notions of righteousness. Already within the Hebrew Scriptures—both the Writings and the Prophets—we see a more beautiful vision: *the righteousness of radical inclusion*.

Ruth and Boaz: We have the romantic story of Ruth and Boaz. Ruth, a widow, is considered righteous for her faithfulness to her Jewish mother-in-law. She commits to making Naomi's people her own and worships Naomi's God.

Ultimately, she is remarried to Boaz, a "kinsmen redeemer" who is a type of Christ. Ruth will be the grandmother of King David. But wait: she's a Moabite! A forbidden marriage! And

Radical Inclusion

under the Law, not only can she never enter the assembly, neither should her children for ten generations—including King David! But no—God *includes* Ruth and David and inspires all Israel to embrace their story. Even more amazing, they both show up in Jesus' royal genealogy. Talk about subverting exclusion!

Isaiah's Temple: Isaiah was a Levitical priest, serving faithfully in God's temple when he first saw God (Isa. 6) and was commissioned as a prophet.

His vision of inclusion is truly radical. Scandalous even!

> And let not the foreigner who joins the LORD say,
> "The LORD has kept me apart from His people,"
>   nor let the eunuch say,
> "Why, I am a withered tree."
> For thus says the LORD:
> Of the eunuchs who keep My Sabbath,
>   and choose what I desire
>   and hold fast to my covenant,
> I will give them in My house and within My walls
>   a marker and a name better than the sons and
>   daughters, an everlasting name will I give them
>   that shall not be *cut off* [Isaiah's dark humor].
> And the foreigners who join the LORD
>   to serve Him and to love the LORD's name,
>   to become servants to Him,
>   all who keep the Sabbath, not profaning it
>   and hold fast to My covenant,
> I will bring them to My holy mountain

> and give them joy in My house of prayer.
> Their burnt offerings and sacrifices
> > shall be welcome on My altar.
> For My house shall be called a house of prayer
> > for all the peoples.
> > —Isaiah 56:3-7

This breathtaking vision imagines those who've been excluded under the Levite Law streaming in—those of other nations, those who've been segregated by birth, those who've been castrated—and they are not only entering the temple to worship in the outer courts (as in the Gospels). They are serving in the temple, offering sacrifices at the altar! They are included with all the privileges of the Jewish sons and daughters—with a Name *even better* than theirs!

Jesus rejects temple exclusion: Immediately after Jesus' triumphal entry, the weekend prior to his death, he proceeds to his *Abba's* house—the temple. He overthrows the tables of the moneychangers and drives out the animals from the Court of the Nations. He recalls those same words from Isaiah 56 and occupies the temple over the course of the week. His Passion Week teachings in the temple were prophetic and provocative. He envisions the destruction of the temple and he scolds the priesthood. And he heals people. Lots of people! People who, because of their physical condition are considered unclean—but there they are—with Jesus, in the temple, being healed and included.

There we have it: these exclusionary Levitical laws on the one hand and the visions of Isaiah the prophet on the other.

Radical Inclusion

The prophets see a better world—those who, by the Spirit of God, imagine a righteousness of radical engagement and inclusion that looks like the river flowing from the temple across boundaries and to all nations. The turn from eradication and exclusion under Moses to inclusion and engagement through Isaiah's visions and Jesus' fulfillment is a dramatic hinge in the history of our faith. That difference will become the bold hyphen in the compound term, "Judeo-Christian."

FIRST CENTURY WARNING

No stranger is to enter
within the balustrade round
the temple and enclosure.
Whoever is caught
will be himself responsible
for his ensuing death.

MEADOWVALE WELCOME

We extend a special welcome to those who are single, married, divorced, widowed, LGBTQ, confused, filthy rich, comfortable or dirt poor.

We extend a special welcome to wailing babies and excited toddlers.

We welcome you whether you can sing like Pavarotti or just growl quietly to yourself. You're welcome here if you're just browsing, just woken up or just got out of prison. We don't care if you're more Christian than the Archbishop of Canterbury, or haven't been to church since Christmas ten years ago.

IN: INCARNATION & INCLUSION

We extend a special welcome to those who are over sixty but not grown up yet and to teenagers who are growing up too fast. We welcome keep-fit moms, football dads, starving artists, tree-huggers, latte-sippers, vegetarians, junk-food eaters. We welcome those who are in recovery or still addicted. We welcome you if you're having problems, are down in the dumps, or don't like 'organized religion.'

We offer a welcome to those who think the earth is flat, work too hard, don't work, can't spell, or are here because Grannie is visiting and wanted to come to church.

We welcome those who are inked, pierced, both or neither. We offer a special welcome to those who could use a prayer right now, had religion shoved down their throat as kids, have lived in Canada their whole lives or just arrived yesterday.

We welcome pilgrims, tourists, seekers, doubters ... and YOU!

What a contrast! And by the way, times are changing. I've visited a modern synagogue just as welcoming as Meadowvale. Check out this Jewish community in Miami:

WELCOME TO BETH OR

Welcome to Beth Or where tradition and a reimagined Judaism come together. We are beginning a new chapter at Beth Or to reimagine the conversations on what makes Judaism relevant and meaningful.

Radical Inclusion

> We are reimagining ...
> - what it means to create sacred space.
> - our ancient texts and traditions in order to breathe new life into making them meaningful for our lives and for our families.
> - how Judaism can inform our response to social issues that plague our world.
> - how to be more intentional about creating a world with mended relationships, civil discourse, respect and love for one another.
> - how we can draw deeper inspiration and gratitude from our life's journey.
>
> We invite you, whatever your religious background gender, sexual orientation or God belief, to join us as we reimagine a renewed sense of purpose for the coming year ... together.

Beautiful! At what point do the people of God make that sharp corner? How were they transformed from zealous exclusionists into radical inclusivists? From violent threats for trespassing to open-door invitations?

CORNELIUS' CONVERSION: RADICAL INCLUSION ESTABLISHED

This brings us to the story of Cornelius in the book of Acts, where the apostle Peter—one of these zealous exclusionists—has his wake-up call.

It's 2005, and I'm in Llanelli, Wales, with my dear friends, Mark and Karen Lowe. They've invited me to speak on Christ's all-inclusive embrace at Antioch Church, a faith community that embodies this message in their city.

After my talk on Sunday morning, an old-style charismatic with a warm heart approached me with this message:

> As I listened to you talk about the way Christ has opened up his temple and his table, I felt concerned. I found your radically open invitation troubling. I started objecting, "But Lord, *you* said this and that in your Word! [meaning the Bible]
>
> At that point, Peter's vision in Acts 10 came into my mind. I remembered how Peter saw a great sheet descending from heaven, full of unclean things. When the Lord told him, "Take and eat," Peter was shocked. He objected, "No, Lord! I've never eaten anything unclean!" He *knew* what the Law—*God's Law*—said about such things. He was confident that he knew God's final word on the matter. And God rebuked Peter: "Do not call anything impure that God has declared clean." Just then, some "unclean" Gentiles knocked at his door. Peter got the message.
>
> I felt that God was telling me, "I'm doing a new thing as in the days of Peter, the blanket and my open door to the Gentiles. It is not as though I did not give this word in the first place, but this is a new season.
>
> *"The blanket is coming down again.* And you will be as shocked as Peter because you *are* godly and you *do* know my word. You will say, 'But Lord, *you* said . . .' But I am the Lord and while I do not change, I reserve the

Radical Inclusion

> right to change you—to change your heart and your eyes—to change how you see my plans for this season."

As jarring as a wider mercy was to this congregant, imagine Peter! And imagine his congregants! Peter's vision and Cornelius' conversion marked a landmark turning point in the history of the people of God, so much so that Luke will record the events twice, narrating both Cornelius' and Peter's experience, then repeating the story's essential details through Peter's own testimony.

Peter, an eyewitness of the risen Christ.

Peter, the one who had heard the great commission, "Go to *all* nations."

Peter, who still refused to eat with Gentiles. How is he going to make that corner? How will he help God's people see it? He tells us in Acts chapter 11:

> When he went up to Jerusalem, some of the circumcised disputed with him. "You went indoors with men who have foreskins!" [How does it keep coming back to that?] And not only that, you ate with them. But Peter explained to them from the beginning, saying, "I was in the city of Joppa, praying. And in an ecstasy, I saw a vision: a certain shape, descending like a great sheet, having been let down from the sky by four corners. And it came right up to me. Gazing into which I perceived and saw the quadrupeds of the earth, the wild beasts and the birds of the sky, And I heard a voice saying to me, 'Get up, Peter. Sacrifice and eat.' And I

said, 'Certainly not Lord, for nothing profane or impure has ever entered my mouth.' And the voice answered a second time out of the sky, 'Do not deem profane what God has made pure.' And this happened three times and everything was lifted into the sky again. [Did you notice the three denials... again? *Déjà vu*]. And see, all at once, three men were standing at the household where I was, having been sent to me from Caesarea. And the Spirit told me to go with them, hesitating at nothing, and these six brethren came with me as well and came into the man's house. And he recounted to us how he had seen the angel standing in his house and saying, 'Send to Joppa and summon Simon who is also called Peter who will speak words to you by which you may be saved, you and all your household.' And as I began to speak, the Spirit, the Holy One, fell upon them as upon us also at the beginning. And I remembered the word of the Lord, how he said, 'John indeed baptized in water but you will be baptized in the Holy Spirit.' So, if God gave them a gift equal to the one he also gave us when we had faith in the Lord Jesus, the Anointed One, who was I that I might hinder God." And hearing these things they quieted down and gave glory to God saying, "then God has also given the nations turning of the heart toward life."

—Acts 11:2-18 (DBH)

Thanks be to God! So, here we have Cornelius *before Christ*.

Radical Inclusion

CORNELIUS' FAITH PRACTICES

In this account, we see some amazing affirmations of this man prior to faith in Christ. We have God's validation of Cornelius' pre-Christian faith practices. For example, the text in chapter 10 says he was *devout*. That means he was deeply committed, faithful, a devoted man. And he *revered* God—and not just any god. Not the god of his own imagination. He wasn't the pope of his own self-made religion. Rather, he seems to *fear* God, *honor* God, *worship* the God of Abraham. We suppose this because the Jews are mightily impressed by him. The Jewish people in his community had seen his life, his spirituality and his godly practices and they had identified him as a "God-fearer." He was an outsider, yes, but one who believed in and worshiped the God of Abraham—our God and Jesus' *Abba*.

Moreover, we read that he donated generously to the poor—he was an almsgiver. Do you remember when Jesus said, "Do not lay up treasures for yourselves on earth, where moth and rust corrupt, but lay up treasures for yourselves in heaven." Store up treasures in heaven. How do you do that?

In the Jewish world and even in the Sermon on the Mount (Matt. 5-7), that is done through almsgiving—that is, giving gifts to the poor. And this man was an almsgiver. Not only did he donate generously to the poor, but the text says that *"God saw it and remembered."* God *noticed* his generosity, noticed his treatment to the poor.

We also read that Cornelius was continually praying. He not only prayed, but the Bible says God *heard* those prayers, which is quite amazing.

IN: INCARNATION & INCLUSION

Cornelius before Christ

Here is a man who is not yet a Christian, yet God notices and affirms his treatment of the poor as an act of righteousness. And God hears his prayers from heaven.

Then, when *Abba* begins to communicate with Cornelius, at every single stage, prior to his conversion, Cornelius is zealous to obey. He hears the Voice and carefully follows what the Word says. Cornelius is "the wise man who," as Christ said, "builds his house upon the rock."

To summarize his God-affirmed faith practices, Cornelius:

- Is devout (faithfully committed)
- Reveres God
- Donates generously
- Continually prays
- Practices obedience

CORNELIUS' SPIRITUAL EXPERIENCES

Cornelius not only has God-affirmed faith practices; he also has God-initiated spiritual experiences. His spiritual repertoire is impressive for someone who does not yet identify as a Christian. He's having visions—as profound and authentic as any of the prophets, such as Isaiah or John the Baptist—*prior* to his conversion to Christ. Prior to his revelation of the beautiful gospel.

And not only visions! He experiences angelic visitations like those you read about in the Prophets. Yes, Cornelius interacts with an angel of the living God! This angel delivers words from the Lord, direct messages from God to Cornelius.

Radical Inclusion

Is this possible? Can people hear God's voice before they come to Christ? Cornelius did. And in fact, he was getting revelations that included specific addresses and names! Not bad! Normally, if I hear a specific "word from the Lord," I find myself on the wrong street corner talking to the wrong person. Not so with Cornelius.

"Here's the man you're going to meet, and his name is Simon [Peter]. And you're going to meet him at this other man's house, Simon the tanner." He even knows Simon's exact vocation.

Cornelius was experiencing upper-level, authentic revelation. Also, we read about third-party revelations delivered to the preeminent apostle in that world about him. That would be like me getting a phone call from the Pope in Rome or the Ecumenical Patriarch in Istanbul saying, "Brad, I had a world-changing revelation last night. It was a dream about you and God gave me your cell number."

What would that say to me? Today, I think it would tell me I need to get off-grid from the ever-listening Siri, Facebook or NSA! But for Cornelius, it meant, "Wow, I'm on God's radar!"

Let's summarize Cornelius' God-initiated spiritual experiences. Cornelius had:

- Visions
- Angelic visitations
- Messages from God
- "Words of knowledge"
- Third-party revelations

IN: INCARNATION & INCLUSION

If the church's founding apostle, St. Peter, is receiving revelations about Cornelius, you know Cornelius is on God's radar. If Cornelius is having such profound and authentic spiritual encounters, he's been noticed in heaven. Would that we all took Jesus more seriously when he said, "God notices sparrows falling! So he notices you too!" Grandiosity not required! On the other hand, now *Abba* sure had Cornelius' attention.

BEFORE CHRIST?

All of this is before Christ. Or is it? Actually, **no one** *is ever before Christ* (chronologically). Because *we are **all** ever before Christ* (always on his mind!). In other words, no one's spiritual journey predates the Cross.

Where does your journey begin? Every spiritual journey that leads to the waters of eternal life began way before we first say "Yes" to Jesus. That journey began the first time Jesus said his "Yes" to you in the eternal counsels of God, then united with you and the rest of the human race in his Incarnation.

Romans 5 is so important on this topic:

- *When you were weak, he died for you.*
- *When you were a sinner, he forgave you.*
- *When you were his enemy, Christ reconciled you to himself.*

And all that happened to you long ago when the curse of Adam was undone through the revelation of Jesus Christ. This is the gospel: that Christ died for the *world*.

Radical Inclusion

Before we ever heard of him.
Even when we were antagonistic to him.

Your spiritual journey

When did your spiritual journey begin? When you believed in Christ? When you were born? How about 2000 years ago (and from all eternity) through the work of Jesus Christ? *There is no before Christ because you were ever before Christ.* You have always been on his radar.

From all eternity, you were in his heart and mind. And you've been carved on the palms of his hands. With real nails!

Cornelius' story—the validation of his faith practices and his spiritual experiences—is rooted in the work of Christ, in the Incarnation.

Peter comes awake to this. Peter gives us his eyewitness confirmation that this guy is *IN. And already was. When* does he come in? We've got these phrases:

- "Do not deem profane what God *has made pure.*"

That's before his baptism. God has made him pure. Already? It's worse than that!

- "We must not call *any man* profane or impure."

We must not deem anyone an outsider or outlier. We must begin to see that what Christ did, he did for *all* and in that sense, they're already *IN*.

- "In every people, *whoever* reveres God and performs works of righteousness is accepted by God."

This is challenging. He was *already cleansed and accepted* by

God? Wait ... what? But we didn't even get him "saved" yet!

That brings us to a crisis. But let's not exit the story prematurely into easy pluralist assumptions.

What are Peter's takeaways?

- *They are in! Exclusion is over.*
- *No one is unclean. God makes no distinction. Neither can we.*
- *Everyone has been accepted, cleansed and included through the work of Jesus Christ.*
- *But then what? Therefore?*

Yes, Peter's takeaways include an all-important *therefore*.

RIPE FOR "THIS ONE"

I love this part. Is Peter's conclusion that Cornelius' authentic faith practices and spiritual experiences preclude the gospel? Does he think, "Oh, it's okay. God has affirmed his faith and righteousness. No need to bring Jesus into the conversation."

Is that what Peter thinks? No. His discovery of *radical inclusion* is not apart from Christ and the gospel but because of it. The *radical uniqueness* of Christ makes the gospel's *radical inclusion* possible and actual.

Peter sees in Cornelius a spiritual, righteous man—his faith already conceived in Christ, now developed to full term—ready for the waters of baptism to break in new birth. Ready for a midwife-witness to introduce Cornelius to the fullness and face of the God he's already been worshiping. What occurs to Peter is that Cornelius' faith is ripe for the revelation

Radical Inclusion

of Christ and the good news of the gospel. His faith practices and spiritual experiences were all for "this One."

And now the text gives us the content of Peter's gospel (Acts 10:37-43)—how he testifies to "this One"—Jesus Christ.

- "*This one*—Jesus—is Lord of everyone!"
- "*This one* God raised up on the third day!"
- "*This one* God marked out as judge of the living and the dead."
- "*To this one* all the prophets bear witness: everyone having faith in him is to receive forgiveness through his name."
- While still uttering these words, the Spirit, the Holy One, the Gift was poured out on *ALL* those listening ... and [they] were baptized.

As Peter shared the gospel about Jesus Christ with Cornelius—before these 'outsiders' could even respond—the Holy Spirit falls on them. And Peter is like, "Whoa, the Holy Spirit is falling on them! Trinity is doing it all backward! Quick! Get some water! He's obviously already IN, so we need catch up and baptize them."

In short, Peter sees Cornelius' inclusion as the reason to share the good news of Jesus Christ—not an excuse to neglect it. Cornelius' spiritual pregnancy in Christ has come full-term and he's "born from above."

What an amazing, beautiful welcome story of inclusion! What an affirmation of every mile of our faith journey! What a reminder that Christ is the *radically unique* author, revelation and fulfillment of *Abba's radical inclusion.*

IN: INCARNATION & INCLUSION

COMMUNITY REFLECTION

I'm a big proponent of the Jewish and Anabaptist practice of community hermeneutics—i.e., interpreting the Scriptures and weighing our reflections *together*. I've been working with the Cornelius story since I first read it in elementary school, then when I first taught it (four times) at a Mennonite college in 1996-97. More recently, I tested the broader implications of this inclusion at *Word of Life Church* in Missouri as part of a series with Brian Zahnd. When old ideas are new to me, I know I need to work them out in community with wise and seasoned practitioners.

Most recently, I worked them over with Bruxy Cavey and some of his staff (Rebecca Thomson and Jimmy Rushton) at *The Meeting House* in Mississauga on their "After Party" podcast titled "What is Evangelism?" The interview featured affirmation, healthy pushback and new (to me) insights.

I found it so helpful that I'll tease the podcast (broadcast May 15, 2019) with these relevant excerpts from the transcript. I'll pick it up just after I've discussed Peter's assertion that "In every people, whoever reveres God and performs works of righteousness is *accepted* by God."

Bruxy: This is good stuff. Let me push back. You've said that Cornelius was already accepted by God. What about Isaiah 64 that says, "All our righteousness is as filthy rags." They're really an insult to God. Don't even try to pray or do good deeds because . . . not only do you need to repent of your sin but even your good deeds are just an insult to God. How do we

Radical Inclusion

compare that word to Israel in Isaiah 64 with this idea of Cornelius in Acts chapter 10, having his good deeds and his prayers rising to God as pleasing incense?

Brad: Either Acts is correcting Isaiah—I don't think that's what's happening—or we shouldn't have totalized Isaiah. Perhaps in context we could hear the righteous deeds and acts—"all *your* righteousness is"—is like Christ's critique of the Pharisees. He's not saying, "Everybody in the world who does good things needs to know that your good things are worthless." Acts clearly contradicts that idea and we would even say that Acts is a fuller revelation of the truth of it. Acts absolutely affirms good deeds and works. So what happened in Isaiah? Likely in context, he's critiquing their acts while [in truth] they weren't righteous at all.

Bruxy: Yes, I'm with you there. Let me read Isaiah, because this is a classic verse that's quoted as a soundbite in many contexts and then used as the paradigm for interpreting all good deeds everywhere at all times, where even our good deeds are seen as filthy rags...

Rebecca: Which Paul reiterates in Romans...

Bruxy: Yes, and he says, "No one does good" based on Psalm 14. In Romans 3, he says, "There's no one who does righteousness" but in Psalm 14, "No one doing good" is contrasted with "those who do righteousness." So Psalm 14 is not totalizing: he contrasts those who don't do good with those who do righteousness within the same Psalm.

Now going back to Isaiah 64, just to read it in context, he

says, speaking of God, "You come to help those who gladly do right and who remember your ways." First of all, he believes there are those who gladly do right—that sounds like Acts 10— "God comes to those who gladly do right and remember your ways ... but when WE continued to sin against them, you were angry. How then can we be saved?"

So he says there are people out there, maybe even the Gentiles, who are doing right and you're willing to help them. But when we continue to sin—*continue* to sin—of course you're angry. How then can we be saved? For all of *us* have become like one who is unclean and all *our* righteous acts are like filthy rags. So even in this passage, he's not totalizing but comparing those of us who are religious hypocrites, and all our actions are just increasing our religious hypocrisy. But already, just a verse earlier, he says there are those out there who are doing well and God receives them. So it's amazing how totalizing one verse can be when the verse just before it says there are people out there like Cornelius. It's so beautiful.

A little later in the interview...

Bruxy: This connects with something I've observed in Jesus' teaching about the sheep and the goats in Matthew 25. When the sheep are welcomed into glory with Jesus, he doesn't say, "You're here because you did good deeds. Period. Therefore, you earned your way in." He says, "You're here because you did this to me." And so it is still because of their honor of Jesus. Jesus still is the way, the truth and the life, even for the sheep who didn't know Jesus was the way, the truth and the life. It is not that Jesus saves some people by grace and other people through works. It is that the grace of Jesus is applied to those people [who didn't know their works were for him]—but it's still Jesus who saves the sheep. He just says, "You expressed your faith in me without knowing it is me."

Rebecca: He's interpreting their love for others as love for himself.

Bruxy: Right, which is a theme throughout Scripture. It's so interesting that in the Gospels, Jesus gives two commandments: "Love God with everything you've got and love others as yourself" and then that's never repeated by the apostles. All that's repeated by the apostles and the rest of the New Testament is to love others. Just love others. Go straight to the love others part and you fulfill the whole Great Commandment. The early church just knew the way we're going to love God is through loving others around us.

THOUGHTS

1. If Jesus Christ is the same yesterday, today and forever (Heb. 13:8) and if he's the fullness of the image of God (Col. 2:9), it's striking that the Bible sometimes presents righteousness as violent exclusion and other times as loving inclusion. How do we account for these conflicting notions? What revelation does each perspective carry? Are there ways they can't both be true? Are there times when each is true in its own way?

2. Under the New Covenant, us-them and in-out dualisms collapse into an all-inclusive invitation. In our day, where do these Christless dualisms persist? Who is the malignant other I keep out, whether overtly or subtly? How would the gospel

of radical inclusion address that in me? Where would it knock on the door of my faith community? What sheet needs to come down again?

3. Under the Law, blending religions was considered idolatrous. How does syncretism continue to be dangerous to the Christian faith? Does Isaiah's vision in chapter 56 or *Abba's* affirmation of Cornelius' faith practices and spirituality slip into syncretism? If not, why not?

4. If Cornelius is already considered righteous, clean and accepted by *Abba* through Jesus, why was it necessary for Peter to share the gospel? What were the "value-added" benefits of hearing and receiving his message? More on that later.

PRAYERS

Abba, I am grateful that you were thinking of me and walking with me long before I acknowledged you. Thank you for conceiving me in love before I had conceptions of you. Thank you for patiently ripening me in the womb of faith prior to my birth from above. Thank you for seeing my faith practices and spiritual experiences as good-faith steps toward Abba's house rather than simply negating my faith quest. And thank you for the witness of Grace and her messengers—I for one am grateful to have met Jesus. He's the most radically unique Person I've ever met.

RADICAL INTIMACY
my *Abba*

WHERE I CAME TO in the Cornelius story is that Peter's engagement with Cornelius reveals the good news of *Abba's radical inclusion* and leads to preaching the good news of *Christ's singular uniqueness*. These two facets of the *Way* are not contradictory if in his own Person,

- *Christ is the unique mediator of Abba's all-inclusive love* (i.e., Christ brings *Abba* to us), and
- *Christ is the unique mediator of intimacy with Abba* (i.e., Christ brings us to *Abba*).

MERCY

My breakthrough in seeing the relationship of *Abba's* radical inclusion and Christ's radical uniqueness came via a word of wisdom from my friend Mercy Aiken. My specific question is how, amid all this talk of *Abba's* all-inclusive love, we are to read John 14:6: "I am the way, the truth and the life. Nobody comes to *Abba* except through me."

Mercy is in regular conversation with Jewish and Muslim dialogue partners who consider her their friend. They know the issues well enough to be very familiar with that Bible verse. They've often experienced it as a bludgeon and a deal-killer. In view of her inclusive and gracious friendship, they have asked her how she reads it—and so did I.

She put it this way (as I understand it and am adapting it. Any errors are mine).

KNOWING GOD THROUGH NAMES

All through the ages, people have known God through different **names** [i.e., monikers]. The names they used were not comprehensive but neither were they superfluous. The names used for God were good-faith expressions and revelations of their experience of and relationship with God. God welcomed and embraced these devout, generous, prayerful people through those names. God knew them and loved them. And because God knew them, they could know God through many such names.

Theologian Olivier Clement saw this a generation ago: "From all eternity, God lives and reigns in glory. Each ray of that glory is a divine name and these names are innumerable" (Olivier Clement, *The Roots of Mysticism*, 28).

So when Jesus says, Nobody comes to *Abba* except through me, does he literally mean that nobody prior to Christ had ever known God? Is he saying that Abraham—the "friend of God"—did not know God? How about Moses—with whom God spoke "face-to-face"? And David—the "man after God's own heart"? Nobody in all history ever had a relationship with God prior to Jesus? No, that can't be right.

At some point, there's this incredible shift. Where God had simply been distant, powerful and frankly, scary, he enters a covenant friendship with Abraham. That's new and amazing, even if otherwise unknown. And the plan is that through Abraham and his "seed" (Jesus—Gen. 12:7, Gal. 3:16), all nations would likewise be blessed.

And again, God reveals himself to Moses. It's another breakthrough in revelation. Far better than the almighty and mysterious I AM WHO I AM that we remember. When Moses begs to see God's *glory*, God promises to reveal his *goodness*.

> "I will make all My goodness pass before you, and I will proclaim the Name [the character of his Person] of the Lord before you. I will be gracious to whom I will be gracious, and I will have compassion on whom I will have compassion."
> —Exodus 33:19

The next day, God shows Moses his backside—or better: he shows his prophet what follows behind God. The glory and goodness of God's wake is his **Name**:

> "The Lord, the Lord God, compassionate and gracious, slow to anger, and abounding in lovingkindness and truth; who keeps lovingkindness for thousands [of generations], who forgives iniquity, transgression and sin; yet He will by no means leave [guilt] unpunished, visiting the iniquity of fathers on the children and on the grandchildren to the third and fourth generations."
> —Exodus 34:6-7

Do you see it? God's **Name** (his Person)—I AM—is not abstract philosophy. It is deeply relational. God's **Name** is

Radical Intimacy

I AM compassionate, patient, loving, kind and forgiving. Even the promise to 'punish' is not a threat—it's the two-fold assurance that the consequences of sin only extend a few generations while God's loving care reaches to eternity. Further to that, his care includes making things right when we've been wronged. We need to read the whole paragraph as "God is Love."

That was new territory. Dramatically so! People had never conceived of God or known him that way (except perhaps Hagar). And few would for a long time. But the Abrahamic name of God as *friend* is now also the Mosaic God who is *gracious* and *compassionate*—the God who hears our groans, takes notice (Exod. 2:24) and comes down to deliver (Exod. 3:8).

Then comes David. Mercy Aiken reminded me that the shepherd-king began to call God by many new names, also reflecting his experience. What's special is how many of these names are preceded by the possessive pronoun "MY." My God. God is my king. God is my shepherd. My strong tower. My rock. My fortress. My deliverer.

Through David's revelation, God becomes much more accessible and personal as *my God*. God is no generalized deity out there, up in the heavens. He is more than the terrifying, radioactive glory of Sinai. Through David, we now know God is *my* God—and *our* God. David composes Psalms for his community so they will join him in worshiping God together as their own. This is more than tribal religion claiming to have a monopoly on God. It was about relating to a God who knows each person's heart and cares for them deeply.

In fact, David catches prophetic glimpses of the unique revelation of Christ in his Psalms. We hear occasional poetic references to God as "father of the fatherless" (Ps. 68:5) and of his father-like compassion on his children (Ps. 103:13). But the Father motif is mainly reserved for prophecies extending David's reign through a promised Messiah:

> "He said to me: 'You are My son. I Myself today did beget you.'"
> —Psalm 2:7

> "He will cry to Me, 'You are my Father, My God, and the rock of my salvation.' I also shall make him My firstborn, the highest of the kings of the earth."
> —Psalm 89:26-27

Likewise, Isaiah will regard God as Father of creation (Isaiah 9:6) and Founder of Israel (Isaiah 64:8). He prays, "You, LORD, are our Father, our Redeemer of yore is Your name" (Isa. 63:16). But in context, the prophet is complaining. He recalls God's fatherly/kingly acts of deliverance in the past and questions why he fails to help them now.

Like David, Isaiah envisions God's forthcoming deliverance revealed and fulfilled through a kingly Son who will personalize, universalize and internalize our knowledge of God as divine and intimate *Abba*.

Note the difference between God seen as national Father (rendered *pater* in the LXX) and the more intimate *Abba* (Papa) in the Gospels. Christ alone discloses *Abba* from the bosom of the Father and through the Spirit of Sonship. Today, we cry out, "My *Abba*" in the afterglow of that revelation.

Radical Intimacy

Thus, while there are occasional references to God as Father before Christ, the *Abba* revelation finds its singular locus in the corresponding revelation of Christ as firstborn Son.

Finally, every glimpse of God is fulfilled in the Incarnation of Christ, *Abba's* "only begotten Son," who bears the Spirit of divine Sonship. Christ validates previous ways of knowing God, such as the faith of Abraham or the covenant of Moses, but he then takes us in much closer. For Christ, God is *my Father*. My *Abba*. Through *Abba's* one unique Son, those who follow the *Jesus Way* will know God as *my Abba* too. Christ tells his disciples, "When praying, pray like this: 'Our *Abba*.'"

What Mercy discovered was that when she shared the revelation of intimacy and access to *Abba,* revealed in the unique Sonship of Jesus Christ and offered to the whole world, her Jewish, Christian and Muslim friends alike become very interested in Jesus. Why? Because all devoted believers of the Abrahamic faiths want to know the God of Abraham more intimately.

CHRIST'S UNIQUE MISSION

"Jesus Christ is how we know God.
We know God as love and is love through Jesus Christ."
—Lazar Puhalo

This is the unique mission and gift of Jesus Christ: to reveal the Name (the character of the Person) of God as *Abba* and the nature of *Abba* as Love. In John's version of the Last Supper, Christ lays out this mission explicitly:

1. Christ identifies the central element of his unique

mission as the revelation of God's name, his character, his nature—namely, *Abba:*

> "I revealed your Name *[Abba]* to the people you gave me out of the world..."
> —John 17:6

> "Holy *Abba,* keep them in your Name *[Abba],* the Name *[Abba]* you've given to me, so that they may be one, just as we are one. When I was with them, I kept them in your Name, the Name you've given me.
> —John 17:11-12

2. Christ is *Abba's* Word through whom we know *Abba* as Love *in us* (17:6-7):

> "Righteous *Abba,* even the world didn't know you. But I have known you, and these ones have known that you sent me. I made your name *[Abba]* known to them—yes, and I will make it known; so that the love with which you loved me may be in them, and I in them."
> —John 17:25-26

> "If anyone loves me," Jesus replied, "they will keep my word. My *Abba* will love them, and we will come to them and make our home with [or 'in'] them."
> —John 14:23

3. Christ is the *Abba's* Way—the Straight Path—to knowing God as *Abba* (Jn. 14:6):

> "I am the way," replied Jesus, "and the truth and the life! Nobody comes to *Abba* except through me."
> —John 14:6

Radical Intimacy

4. Christ's love union with *Abba*—their mutual indwelling—and Christ's love union with humanity enables Christ and his *Abba* to live in us.

> "I am praying that they may all be one-just as you, *Abba*, are in me, and I in you, that they too may be in us, so that the world may believe that you sent me."
> —John 17:21

Reflecting on the role of the Holy Spirit in our relationship with *Abba*, Paul will tell the Romans that through Christ, we have "received the spirit of sonship, in whom we call out '*Abba*, Father!'" (Rom. 8:15).

All that to say, even those who already know God's radical inclusion find that Christ is radically unique in his revelation of *Abba* as love, his relationship with *Abba* as mine and his Way to union with *Abba* within. No longer need we think of the God in heaven to be feared—in Christ, we now know God as "our *Abba*, who loves us and lives in us!"

PAPUCHI

As I was learning all this, I made some new friends in Miami—a couple of highly effective counselors with *Hope for Life Ministries:* Lakhi and Giovanna Dadlani. After hearing their powerful redemption story, I noticed the way Giovanna addresses God in prayer. She calls him *Papuchi*, the Spanish equivalent to *Abba* or Papa, but it's even more intimate in that it also implies "mine." *Papuchi*—MY Papa.

Giovanna says, "When I sit down to breakfast, I like to set out an extra placemat for my Papa—for Papuchi. At first, I also needed an icon to give him a face and remind me he was there. But now, whenever I pray to Papuchi, that sense of "mine" assures me that I am already on his lap and in his arms."

That's what I'm talking about: that intimacy with *Abba* was Christ's unique gift to her.

THE NAME(S?) ABOVE EVERY NAME

"Everyone who calls on the **Name** of the Lord will be saved."

Excellent. But which name?

Even at our most conservative, we are still working with at least two **Names** (and not just two monikers, but two Persons): *Abba* and Jesus Christ. Which should we focus on?

In Philippians 2, Paul writes that "at the **Name of Jesus**, every knee will bow and tongue confess that Jesus Christ is Lord." He adds that Christ has been "given the **Name** that is above every name."

What does that mean? Paul could mean that JESUS CHRIST is now the **Name** above every other name. That is, the Person of Jesus has been elevated above all the other names or claims for God.

Or it could mean that *Abba* has conferred on Jesus Christ the divine **Name** already revealed as the most high God: YHWH. To say Jesus is LORD is to identify him as YHWH.

Either way, notice that Jesus Christ IS the **Name** exalted by *Abba* and for *Abba's* glory. Does this negate all other monikers we use for God? No, other names count too.

Radical Intimacy

For example, in prayer, I often address God as *"Abba"* or "Lord." Sometimes I pray, "Father" or "Holy Trinity of Love." Could I also use other names for God from the Bible, such as *"Elohim"* or *"Yahweh"*? How about titles such as "Good Shepherd" or "Lamb of God"?

What if I addressed the Trinity as "Creator God" or "Great Spirit," monikers my Christ-following (and not) First Nations friends prefer?

And other languages? Could I also use the Aramaic word for "Father"—*Abba*—as Jesus did? I obviously do! Jesus told us to, if we take him literally. Surely, the English equivalent *Papa* must also be sanctioned for use in North America and the UK.

So, Aramaic is fine. English is fine. How about German or Spanish? I use the words *Vater* (Father) and *Salvador* (Savior) when worshiping with my friends in Deutschland or Mexico. They appreciate my effort to speak their language. All good.

Now, may I also use the Arabic word for God? Here, some would object. They're offended if I refer to God as *Allah*. God can be *Gott* but he can't be *Allah*, because Muslims call their God *Allah*. Point taken. But wait. Mormons use the words "God" and even "Jesus Christ." Yet I'm probably no more Mormon than I am Muslim. Are those names now forbidden?

How about my friends who attend Alcoholics Anonymous? They talk about *God* or their *Higher Power* a lot, even though many of them staunchly reject Christianity.

Ironically, their *Higher Power* often sounds a lot more like *Abba* than many of the toxic Christian conceptions of God!

IN: INCARNATION & INCLUSION

FACT CHECK

This Name-name or Person-moniker distinction is tricky.

Fact: There are many monikers for God. I use quite a few myself.

Fact: There are many understandings of God. My understanding has grown over time.

Fact: Others use different monikers and have different understandings of God. I don't hold the secret recipe to God stashed in my safety deposit box. Neither do you, do you?

Bible fact: But "everyone who calls on the Name of the Lord"—anyone who reaches out to the divine Person—"will be saved."

More Bible facts: As a Christian, I believe Jesus Christ is Lord, that *Abba* has given him the Name above all names and that when people call on the Name of the Lord, it is Jesus Christ who hears and who answers.

Fact: Many who pray to God disagree. They don't think it's Christ who hears and saves when they call on God. If they are wrong, Christ is still able to hear and save them, isn't he?

Fact: It could be me who's wrong and it wouldn't be the first time. But God's Name and God's Person are not contingent on my monikers or my immature understanding of God.

MANY MONIKERS, ONE NAME
AND THE PERFECT REVELATION

I'm told that Fr. Richard Rohr sometimes closes his prayers with these words: "We pray this in the holy name of Jesus, and all the other holy names of God. Amen."

Radical Intimacy

That got me wondering. What if I said it this way:

Jesus Christ is obviously not the only "holy name" (moniker) of the Lord, even in the Bible. When Peter or Paul use the word "Name," they don't literally mean getting the correct label. The Name is the PERSON to which all the monikers direct our gaze. Thus, Jesus Christ—Creator of all, King of all and Savior of all—is the only Person who perfectly reveals the *Abba* to whom all Holy Names refer.

This is my pushback against religious sectarianism: the gods who are big enough for only one religious moniker, title or sect are too tiny to be Cosmic King and Lord of all lords. Whatever monikers we create to call on the Name of the Lord do not diminish, silence or cripple the Lord's freedom to love, act and save at all.

And here is my pushback against bland pluralism: our particular conceptions of God do affect our Way and Walk in dramatic ways. If I think Ler o' the Sea saved my son, no harm done. Hopefully, a witness such as St. Patrick will arrive to let me know it was Christ who heard and answered.

But if I think Ler demands that I sacrifice my son to the sea, I definitely need a witness to come tell me that's not what Christ wants. Humanity has created a plethora of violent, sacrificial religions (including Christianity) that need to hear of *Abba's* love and learn the *Jesus Way*.

Names are not all created equal and how we understand them matters in day to day life. The difference can be night and day or as Paul says, "darkness and light" (Col. 1:13). Or as Isaiah prophesied, "the people who sat in the dark saw a great light; light dawned on those who sat in the shadowy land of death."

Even though *Abba* loves everyone, not everyone has experienced the liberation found in the Light of the World.

LIGHT OF THE [WHOLE] WORLD

John the Beloved said, "The true light, which gives light to every human being, was coming into the world" (John 1:9). That's radically inclusive.

Jesus adds, "I am the light of the world. Whoever follows me will never walk in darkness, but will have the light of life" (John 8:12). That's radically unique.

I believe Christ's light can shine in any heart, anywhere, at any time. Those who turn to his Light and follow it are turning to Christ and following him, prior even to hearing his moniker, beholding the Cross or understanding his gospel.

The Light that shines is Christ. He will illumine every heart that receives the Light, whether immediately or over time, in this life or the next, when they discover the Light they've been following is the Person of Jesus Christ. Some will say, "Of course! I get it now!" Others will be shocked because of how badly Christendom misrepresented Jesus' name to them.

I believe Christ was right: through his unique Way, we are led into divine intimacy with God as the indwelling *Abba* of Love! Some might wonder at the exclusivity of that claim, but I see no other prophets in any religion offering or delivering the *Abba* relationship.

Radical Intimacy

THOUGHTS

1. When you pray, who do you relate to most strongly? Father, Son or Spirit? What name do you prefer to use when addressing God? Have you found that the name you use influences the quality of your prayers? Why not? Or how so?

2. Do you think God hears the prayers of those of other faiths? How does Paul address this in Acts 17 when speaking to Athenians? Did he believe *Abba* heard their prayers? Could Paul's arrival as a witness to Christ be an answer to their prayers? Could your arrival indicate that someone's Light has summoned you to be a witness to the Name?

3. Is it better to worship and serve the true Light, not knowing his name or to use the name of Jesus liberally while loading it with toxic associations? What if we went for a third way? What if we affirmed the true Light that people have already seen and felt, and then encouraged them to see how that Light also became beautifully incarnate?

PRAYERS

Our Abba, thank you for revealing yourself through the Light, the Word and the Name (Person) of your unique Son, Jesus Christ. Thank you, Jesus Christ, for revealing God as Abba of intimate Love. Thank you, Grace ... Holy Spirit, for coming to make the Holy Trinity of co-eternal Love resident in my heart.

We call on your name, Lord, for a greater revelation of your true nature and pray for that same enlightenment in all your children. Amen.

RADICAL ENGAGEMENT
Toddlers with Crayons

"WE KNOW WHERE SALVATION IS; we don't know where it is not."
—Orthodox maxim

Religious pluralism is an attempt to escape the exclusivism of competing truth claims, but it cannot escape its own exclusivism since the trendy, liberal pluralist excludes discussion on even minimal truth claims.

The question is, will our truth claims be subtle and nuanced or rigid and brittle? Will they be meaningful or crude? Can we speak of a generous common grace for which Christ is the fulfillment of all the great traditions? Will we learn the art of dialogue in today's global village? The common grace/ natural theology tradition, exemplified in Bede Griffiths, is neither pluralistic nor syncretistic but elastic and vibrant.

—Ron Dart

AIRPLANE EVANGELISTS

I was boarding an airplane—a Southwest airlines jet where you board by number but can pick your own seat once you enter the plane. I head down the aisle and secured an excellent aisle seat—14 C—which allows my right arm space in the aisle. If I want to write, I'm not elbowing my neighbor. Someone

Radical Engagement

was in the window seat but so far, the middle seat was empty and I hoped it would stay that way. I start "man-spreading" to supersize myself and look inhospitable.

I'm praying, "Lord, you love me, right? Please just let me be left alone." I overdosed on air transit long ago and I don't much like airplane evangelists. I don't want to be one.

I see this man coming down the aisle. He catches my eye from half a dozen rows away and I know I'm sunk. "Oh no," I pray. "Why me, God? Why do you hate me?" This is a BIG guy. I have wide shoulders and so does he. I'm thinking, "Look bigger! Inhale! Expand! Come on, Brad! BE the pufferfish!"

Nope. The BIG man locks in and proceeds directly to the B seat beside me. "God," I pray, "grant me the serenity to accept what I cannot change," mainly to avoid the panic of knowing we'll be two sardines crammed together for the next five and a half hours.

"Acceptance," I breathe the Serenity Prayer to myself, since God's obviously tuned out. Try to make the most of it, I think. I notice my neighbor is wearing a black robe, nearly identical to the cassock I wear when serving at the monastery.

"I see you're some sort of cleric," I say politely.

"Yes, I am," he replies.

"Welcome here," I lie.

He sees this as an opening and begins to relate some of his spiritual experiences, beginning with this moment.

"Do you believe God still speaks?" he asks, not knowing that I wrote *Can You Hear Me? Tuning In to the God Who Speaks* over fifteen years ago—it has sort of been my shtick.

IN: INCARNATION & INCLUSION

"I do," I reply.

"So do I. I believe in God's voice," he says with enthusiasm. "I believe he guides and directs, counsels and gives wisdom to anyone who asks. And you know what? As I came down the aisle today, I was asking God, 'Who do you want me to sit with?' And he directed me to you."

Sheesh ... airplane evangelists. I said I don't want to be one. But sitting beside one can prove even worse. But I remember the wisdom of an old Welshman—a BBC radio host who interviewed celebrities back in the 1950s. He told me, "Always remember: every person you meet is absolutely fascinating! This will help you listen better and ask the right questions." With that "prompting," I settle into interview mode and I'm happy to report that we entered a beautiful conversation about topics of great interest to me.

I began to ask him about his conceptions of God (a la *A More Christlike God*). I learned this man is devout. He loves God and longs only to be God's faithful servant. He actively prays to God and listens for God's voice. We talked about the power of healthy images of God versus toxic, idolatrous images.

"Here is my image of God," he said. "God is merciful, all-merciful, especially merciful."

"Amen!" I say, a little too loudly.

"I believe that on judgment day, God will reveal himself as just and merciful."

"Amen!" I said again, and we compared strikingly similar visions of restorative justice.

By now it was clear that like me, my new friend is a

preacher, so I asked him how he approaches that task. "What are the essentials of weekly preaching? What are the non-negotiables to your message?"

"Every sermon must be uplifting, inspiring and beautiful," he said, "because our faith is uplifting, inspiring and beautiful."

"Amen, brother!" I said, feeling a little bit bad for the girl boxed into the window seat. She's pretending to be asleep beside two enthusiastic evangelists.

CHRIST-FOLLOWING MUSLIMS

I haven't mentioned yet: my new friend is an Imam. That's right: he's a Muslim missionary who leads a Mosque in the Pacific Northwest.

Our long flight included conversations about God as all-merciful (from the opening line of the Qur'an) and led to our shared conviction that Christians and Muslims alike must reject all violence done in the name of God. We both desire to be peacemakers and bridge-builders in God's kingdom. While our understanding of *Abba* /Allah differs significantly, we both pray to the God of Abraham, the covenant God of Jacob and Ishmael—to the same God who Jesus worshiped and to whom he prayed, "Our *Abba*."

Still, a voice in my ear whispered, "Yeah, but he's one of *them*. And remember, Jesus said, *If you're ashamed of me now, I'll be ashamed of you on judgment day.*" The words are biblical, but the chiding didn't have the tone and texture of God's empowering Spirit. Hey, even Satan can quote Scripture. I knew it was the voice a guilty conscience conditioned by years of awkward and ineffectual "obligation evangelism."

I waved it off, but the nagging persisted, "When are we going to talk about Jesus?"

I thought to myself, *I believe we're going to talk about him right now, but not begrudgingly or under pressure.*

Because I am confident of Christ and his sensitivity to each individual's place and pace on the journey, I try to share my point of view freely without arm-twisting arguments or offensive condescension. The Imam and I share common ground but that doesn't preclude me from also sharing my take on the good news of Jesus Christ.

I finally broached the subject this way: "I am aware of Muslim followers of Jesus who don't convert to Christianity, yet are committed to knowing and obeying Jesus. What do you think of that phenomenon?"

He smiled and said, "Oh yes. I believe in that. I'm a follower of Jesus." He elaborated on what his stream of Islam believes about Jesus.

I know there are impasses to our theology of Jesus. As an Orthodox Christian, I believe that Jesus is God. As a Muslim, he must believe Jesus is not God. But out of pure ignorance, most Christians I know have caricatured Islam by minimizing their belief in Christ, as if they believe he's just one of the prophets. That's sloppy and probably slanderous. It's worth probing who Jesus is to Muslims with actual Muslims (recognizing they are not all on the same page—as if Christians are). Here's what they tell me:

"Jesus was born of the Virgin Mary by the breath of God's

Radical Engagement

Spirit. He is alive. Jesus is the prophet of the Spirit and Allah's Messiah. Jesus is coming again and he's going to overthrow the antichrist and establish God's kingdom on earth. We need to obey Jesus' commandments to love God with our whole heart and treat others as we want to be treated. We need to follow his teachings on the way of peace."

Some Imams, like the one I met on the plane, believe that Christ's return comes not with violence but with a revelation of his Way of peace. The antichrist to be overcome is not some political superstar but the spirit of hatred and violence that rules so much of our hearts and religious movements.

And I thought, "Not bad! I know Christians who couldn't say that." We also openly talked about the deal-breakers—areas where we are not in agreement about the nature of God (as Trinity) or Jesus Christ (as fully divine). When I suggested that being peacemakers is not merely sharing common ground, but includes mutual respect in our differences, the Imam was exuberant. He agreed. He also insisted I visit his home, share a meal with him and he offered his considerable influence to open doors for me around the world should I need his help.

My Imam friend may never see Jesus as I do. He likely won't convert to Christianity. But I believe he will continue to revere God and more specifically, believe in and follow Jesus as he understands him.

I am also sure I'll never convert to Islam. How then shall we relate to each other? I will do my best to share the good news of God's love revealed in Jesus to him and whoever will listen. And Azam does listen—carefully and perhaps even joyfully!

IN: INCARNATION & INCLUSION

TODDLERS WITH CRAYONS

My friend and colleague Dr. Andrew Klager offered me a helpful and faithful reminder for such discussions. When it comes to understanding the transcendent God "who dwells in unapproachable light," even after we receive the revelation of *Abba's* image in Christ and the gift of the Holy Spirit, we're all still pretty much theological toddlers.

Like a toddler drawing his mommy or daddy with blunt wax crayons and poor motor skills, I do my very best to compose a picture of *Abba* as I conceive him. I swell with pride, imagining I've "nailed it," drawing bright squiggles on the only canvas I can find: the panel of a cardboard box where I hunker down. I'm enthusiastic, but also handicapped by the limitations of immaturity—I'm also inordinately self-satisfied. In large script, some of it backwards, I complete my masterpiece with the inscription, "To Daddy [or Mommy, if you prefer], Love Brad. XOXO."

I stand up in my little box and call Daddy, proudly offering my fine-art portrait as a gift of worship.

With great care, *Abba* removes the colored panel from the box and gazes at it with affection I know is meant for me. *Abba* seems very pleased indeed. That warm smile must mean I've replicated him perfectly, right? I am sure that when he looks at my picture, *Abba* must feel as if he's looking in a mirror! He takes my special gift and proudly hangs it on his heavenly refrigerator with a great big happy-face magnet. Obviously, *Abba* intends my artwork to be the prototype for all the other toddlers to mimic. But best of all, I receive a huge

Radical Engagement

bear-hug, and I'm told for the umpteenth time that I'm a dearly loved son.

But then I notice another toddler hard at work with crayons—a Muslim boy named Azam. He's sprawled out in his own little cardboard box. He too has been coloring. I'm disturbed that his picture looks so different than mine. Azam is clearly not concerned with staying faithful to the precise lines of my perfect rendition. I see different shapes, unfamiliar colors and sloppy squiggles. I know for a fact that he's drawn *Abba* poorly. His picture is all wrong! In fact, it's obvious to me that he must be drawing an entirely different god.

Perhaps I shouldn't be surprised, because after all, Azam is one of *them*—one of those deluded and deceived Muslims, right? Small wonder he's strayed badly from my beautifully accurate portrayal of "Daddy." Perhaps we don't have the same Dad at all. We may be friends, but we're not brothers, right? Azam tries to assure me we are brothers, but if our contradictory pictures of *Abba* are any indication...

But wait, what is he doing? He's presenting his gift to *Abba*, too. To my God! To my *Abba*! Well, at least he'll see *Abba's* brow furrow with displeasure. Azam is sure to be in for a stern correction! *Abba* will surely show him that I'm right!

Abba takes Azam's colorful picture, looks it over very carefully and then—breaks into a wide grin! What is *Abba* doing? Why is he putting Azam's picture on the fridge too?

And then those same loving arms scoop up Azam, as if he is a cherished child of *Abba*, just like me! Why would *Abba* do that? What could this mean?

IN: INCARNATION & INCLUSION

WHAT RADICAL INCLUSION MEANS (AND WHAT IT DOESN'T)

- Does this prove Azam's picture of *Abba* is right and mine is wrong or vice versa? (sectarianism)
- Does this prove all pictures of *Abba* are accurate and valid? (pluralism)
- Does this prove no pictures of *Abba* are accurate and valid—proof that we should stop trying to compose pictures altogether? (agnosticism)
- Does this mean that where our pictures agree (our common ground), they are accurate and valid?
- Does this mean that where our pictures disagree (our distinctive convictions), they are inaccurate and invalid?
- Are our disagreements proof there is no *Abba* at all? (atheism)

I doubt it. My answer to this quiz is "none of the above." The questions themselves are little more than common knee-jerk assumptions—false arrivals. They either lead to a watered-down unity, a flaccid faith or a doubled-down dogmatism. Notice all the 'proving' going on in each point.

But Azam and I—each emissaries of our respective (but rarely respectful) faiths—agree that we're called to be faithful witnesses, not argumentative lawyers, of our limited understanding and experience of God. So, let's come at the illustration from a different angle (and Azam may agree):

It is true that before God, we are all theological toddlers.

Radical Engagement

Abba (the true God as God truly is) will always be greater than any human conception of God. Any picture we compose of *Abba* will necessarily fall short of his true nature—immature crayon scribbles compared to the reality of *Abba*.

This is exactly what Muslims mean when they say, *"Allahu Akbar!"—God is greater!* Greater than what? God is greater than anything we say about God. He is wholly/holy other than our pinched notions!

• Despite our competing and immature ideas about God, we believe in a real divine *Abba* who exists and transcends every human conception—*Abba* IS absolute Reality.

• Despite our realization that our convictions are quite immature and incomplete, we nevertheless believe that our desire to know *Abba* —to experience divine Love and bear witness to whatever glimpses we've had of *Abba* are acts of worship. We believe *Abba* both instills and approves these desires as worthwhile and pleasing.

• Despite our acknowledgement that our conceptions of *Abba* are immature but not worthless, we don't regard them all as equally valid or helpful. Indeed, some are toxic to one's soul and dangerous to others' wellbeing. For example, shame- or fear-based faith leads to a deep spiritual illness of the soul. And xenophobic faith coupled with militant fervor led to the death-dealing of the Christian crusades and the violence of ISIS. Azam and I see this corrupt fruit as deep distortions that stand in ugly contrast to the best our traditions can offer.

• Despite our differing convictions about *Abba,* and our commitment to adhering to those differences, Azam and I

IN: INCARNATION & INCLUSION

both believe *Abba* loves us and loves the other, and so may we. That love was not earned through sameness, not the accuracy of our perceptions, nor the beauty of our pictures, but rather, freely given to everyone from the heart of *Abba*. The heart of divine Love is responsive to each of *Abba's* children, prior to any spiritual progress and our obvious lack of it. Remember: Paul insists that "every family in heaven and on earth derives its name" from one and the same divine Father (Eph. 3:14) and that "we are all God's children" (Acts 17:28).

• Despite our common ground, Azam and I have not at all watered down our own faiths to only those points where we share common ground. Some of our common ground is central to both our core convictions (e.g. that *Abba* is merciful and we must be merciful). But our respect for each other does not demand the other to abandon essential commitments where we disagree. We both love and follow Jesus Christ. To love and respect each other as brothers, Azam sees that I cannot deny Christ's deity just as I cannot demand that he affirm it. Nor can I say it doesn't matter what we believe about this. It does. And Azam agrees. It matters. And we can't both be right. How shall we then live?

• Precisely at the point of our non-negotiable, deal-killing differences, we choose neither to ignore them, deny them or assault one another over them. Rather, we follow Jesus together as toddler-brothers to the one *Abba* who receives us both and we hear him say,

"My sons [*Abba* pauses to let that sink in]—*thank you for the worship expressed in these precious pictures. My heart is gladdened*

Radical Engagement

by your love. And now I ask for a deeper worship—that you worship me by loving one another as my children. I ask you not to poke any of my sons or daughters in the eye with your crayons. I ask you to live beyond your little boxes, to visit one another and welcome each other as you would welcome me. You both think you know where salvation is—but you don't know where it isn't.

"Most importantly: the best picture you have of me is not the one you composed, hanging on my refrigerator. My likeness is what you see in the face of your brother. My image stands before you—an icon of the living God."

TWO CONVERSATIONS

I'll wind down this chapter with two more true conversations. I've purposely chosen controversial characters who I respect and with whom I differ. Maturity, after all, is the capacity to hold difference respectfully. The point of sharing these dialogues is not about whether you approve of the characters involved, their faith traditions or their ministries. That's irrelevant to the experiment and frankly, a test of our own character. We aren't testing them—we're going to test ourselves.

First conversation–Billy Graham

Billy Graham had a conversation with Robert H. Schuller (of Crystal Cathedral fame) on his Hour of Power TV broadcast over two decades ago. The interview went viral on YouTube because the twentieth century's most famous evangelist made remarks that seemed to betray his Evangelical message. His critics pounced, decrying him as a heretic and a pluralist, but he never walked back on his assertions. Here's the segment:

Schuller: Tell me, what is the future of Christianity?

Graham: Well, . . . I think there's the body of Christ which comes from all the Christian groups around the world, or outside the Christian groups. I think that everybody that loves Christ or knows Christ, whether they're conscious of it or not, they're members of the body of Christ. And I don't think that we're going to see a great sweeping revival that will turn the whole world to Christ at any time.

What God is doing today is calling people out of the world for his name. Whether they come from the Muslim world, or the Buddhist world, or the Christian world, or the non-believing world, they are members of the body of Christ because they've been called by God. They may not even know the name of Jesus, but they know in their hearts they need something they don't have and they turn to the only light they have. I think they're saved and they're going to be with us in heaven.

Schuller: What I hear you saying is that it's possible for Jesus Christ to come into a human heart and soul and life even if they've been born in darkness and have never had exposure to the Bible. Is that a correct interpretation of what you're saying?

Graham: Yes, it is. Because I believe that. I've met people in various parts of the world, in tribal situations, that have never seen a Bible or heard about a Bible, have never heard of Jesus

Radical Engagement

but they've believed in their hearts that there is a God and they tried to live a life that was quite apart from the surrounding community in which they lived.

Schuller: This is fantastic. I'm so thrilled to hear you say that. There's a wideness in God's mercy.

Graham: There is. There definitely is.

Do you agree with Graham? What did you think of him? Wrong questions! Before we get to better questions, it's time for our second story—another conversation.

Second Conversation–Pope Francis

In April 2018, Pope Francis met with children from the parish of St. Paul of the Cross in Corviale, Italy. During a Q&A time, a little boy named Emanuele approached the microphone but was overcome with emotion and buried his face in his hands.

"Come, come, come," said the Francis.

"I can't do it," replied the child.

"Come to me, Emanuele, and whisper in my ear."

After conferring in whispers for a time, the Pope sent the boy back to his seat. He continued,

"If only we could cry like Emanuele when we have pain in our hearts. He cries for his papa who died. And he had the courage to cry in front of all of us because there is love in his heart for his papa.

"I asked Emanuele permission to reveal his question to the public and he said 'Yes.' [He told me,] 'My papa died a short time ago. He was an atheist but he baptized all four of his children. He was a good man. Is Papa in heaven?'

"It's nice that a son says that about his papa, that he was good.

"It is God who says who goes to heaven. But what is God's heart like for a papa like that? What do you think? A papa's heart—God has a papa's heart.

"And with a papa who was not a believer, but who baptized his children and gave them that gift, do you think Papa would be able to leave him far from himself? Do you think that? [crowd: No] Louder! With courage! [crowd: No!] Does Papa abandon his children? [crowd: No!] Does Papa abandon his children when they are good? [No!]

"There, Emanuele, there is the answer. Papa surely was proud of your papa, because it is easier when one is a believer to baptize his children than to baptize them when you are an unbeliever. Surely this pleased Papa very much. Talk to your Papa, pray for your papa. Thanks, Emanuele, for your courage."

What do you think of Pope Francis? Did you like his answer? Wrong questions! We need to ask far better questions than, "Is that person right or wrong? Do I agree or disagree?"

In light of our toddlers-with-crayons analogy, such questions are not only immature, but they have us nibbling from the wrong tree in Eden yet again.

They smell of Christless religion.

Radical Engagement

BETTER QUESTIONS

What is the Basis of our faith? I propose that the Basis of our faith is not our faith. The Basis of our faith is *Abba's* love. The Basis of our faith is Christ's cruciform love. The Basis of our faith is Grace alone, creating the Way of Life for us to travel. Notice: *Abba,* Christ and Grace—triune Love.

For Graham, the Basis of our faith is "because they've been called by God." For Francis, it was "God has a papa's heart." While both clearly affirm that response matters—they absolutely believe and preach this—they see the Basis for salvation in God's loving character and personal initiative. They have clear ideas about what constitutes a good response, but neither of them imagines our good response saves us. *Abba's* love saves us.

Billy Graham and Pope Francis risked sounding like pluralists only because they start from the same New Testament foundation: salvation is found in *Abba's* love revealed in Christ by Grace alone—and this Love extends to all.

Knowing that, we're ready for better questions. Let's ask them now in our Thoughts and Prayers section.

THOUGHTS

1. What are your conceptions of *Abba?* Why not actually grab some blunt crayons, a sheet of construction paper and draw a picture to hang on *Abba's* fridge? As you offer your gift to *Abba,* how do you sense he responds?

2. When confronted with conflicting images of *Abba,* as

with my Imam friend, what happens in your heart? Do you look for differences with which to argue? Do you avoid arguments by emphasizing common ground? Could you hold differences but respect the other enough to respect their convictions? Could you discuss your convictions freely without fear or hostility? Does someone come to mind as I ask these questions? Can you see the image of God in them? Are you able to regard them as a brother or sister?

3. Graham, Francis and I share common ideas about the Basis of our salvation. We probably articulate them differently. How would you articulate it? Would you focus on *Abba's* love, Christ's work, Grace alone or some combination of triune Love? What is the nature of salvation—the gospel—to which you responded? What gospel would you be willing to ask others to embrace? What response would you be looking for?

PRAYERS

Abba, I confess that my conceptions of you are immature and incomplete. I offer them to you, such as they are, as an act of worship. As best I can, I love you rather than my notions of you. Thank you for whatever understanding you've given me to date. And thanks especially for revealing yourself in Christ. Help me see the ways you reveal yourself in my neighbors—even those of different convictions. Forgive my xenophobia and open my heart to love as you do.

RADICAL ENCOUNTERS
Seven Stories

IN THIS CHAPTER, I'll recount seven more experiences that demonstrate *Abba's* all-merciful, radical inclusion and also bear witness to Christ's unique revelation of *Abba*. In my mind, the power of these stories includes the obvious and necessary marriage of inclusion and uniqueness. Further, these testimonies are important because in at least three of these episodes, the story is not tied off in a neat Christian conversion. They emphasize the journey without prescribing an outcome. In other words, the real spiritual life is an open-ended saga awaiting its final chapter—not a youth group lock-in of shallow certitude. These are stories of real people on their journey today—not prescriptions for what they "should have done" or how it "ought to be." They are who they are. Can we suspend judgment enough to hear them?

ESTHER'S STORY:
THE LIGHT THAT SPEAKS

My name is Esther and I have permission to share this story. Recently, I sat with a young twenty-six-year-old man as his emotions came in tsunami-like waves. He wailed from a very deep place in his heart. Although no words passed between us, I sat in solidarity with him as emotion after emotion

Radical Encounters

erupted—we shared a tender sacred space.

Stanley had tried to commit suicide the evening before. The pain of aloneness was too great. Cutting his own throat felt like a relief from the pain of the loneliness he felt.

Stanley believed he was a "lone wolf and a black sheep." I would constantly hear these words coming from him. He had made an agreement with lies that almost took his life. It needed to be broken.

The truth is that Stanley is one of the sweetest, kindest, funniest guys you could ever meet. If you have the honor of meeting him, you'll feel the sweet presence he carries.

As I sat with Stanley, I wondered if he could see Light in the darkness of what he was feeling. I asked him if he could see it. He said he couldn't. I asked him if the Light were to come to him, what it might look like. Again, he had no answer.

Then I took a risk, turned to him and said, "Stanley, look in my eyes."

He looked.

I asked him, "Stanley, can you see Light in my eyes?"

He responded, "Yes, I can."

"Stanley," I asked, "If that Light could speak, what would the Light say to you."

He paused and said, "It says I am a kind person with a good heart and worthy of belonging and love."

It was my turn to become undone!

"Stanley," I asked, "do you believe that?"

He said he found it hard to believe it, but he'd try.

I asked if he could write down the words he had heard from

the Light, and he agreed. However, to my dismay, Stanley wrote the words, "I am a lone wolf and a black sheep."

I reminded him these words were the lies that almost took his life and I asked him how he'd feel if we burned those words. He agreed.

I lit the paper on fire. We watched silently as letter by letter the words disappeared into smoke and ashes.

"Stanley, those words are gone; we watched them burn," I said. "Now, let's try again. Let's write down the words you heard from the Light in my eyes."

I watched as Stanley wrote—this time it said, "I am a kind person with a good heart. I am worthy of belonging and love."

My heart smiled. He said he felt a little better.

In the coming days, whenever Stanley reverted to the "black sheep and lone wolf," I asked him to remember the words the Light had spoken to him. As the weeks progressed, I watched Stanley's transformation. Over time, the Light overcame the darkness.

Now you'll never hear him say he's a lone wolf or a black sheep. Now you'll hear him say, "Hi, my name is Stanley. I'm a kind person with a good heart and worthy of belonging and love." Now he says he feels like a "member of the world." He found a job and a friend and loves his life.

Light transformed the darkness within, and Stanley believes what he says. He feels the change inside him. He says he feels the Light within.

Stanley is thankful for the Light that speaks. So am I and so is the world as his healing ripples into the Universe.

Radical Encounters

TAI CHI AND ROMANS

My friend, Scott Erickson (AKA @ScottThePainter) told me the story of a friend of his who had been into Tai Chi for three decades. While practicing Tai Chi at a young age, he began to hear a voice speaking to his heart. The Voice was beautiful, good, and peaceful and was one of the main attractions for his Tai Chi practice. He began to recognize the Voice and trust the Voice. After thirty years, the Voice began to say things that reminded him of truths he heard were in the Bible. So, he thought he should pick up a Bible and read it for himself.

I don't know why—maybe at the direction of the Voice—Scott's friend started reading Paul's letter to the Romans. Back in the day, I might have expected Paul's epistle to rebuke him and call him to repent of practicing Tai Chi, since it's connected to non-Christian philosophy and spirituality. But that didn't happen. Instead, he discovered the same Voice he'd been hearing all along in Tai Chi speaking through the inspired words of Paul! Is *Abba* allowed to do that?

Do you see what happened there? He was able to trust the words in Scripture because he had already learned to trust that same Voice during his thirty years of Tai Chi!

How did this work? Was this fellow's approach to Tai Chi his Way of "calling on the name of the Lord"? Or by Grace, could *Abba* have chosen to interpret it that way? "Call on me and I will answer you," says the Lord (Jer. 33:3). And so he did—the Word began to speak to him!

But what if he used the wrong name? What if he had mistaken ideas? Isn't that syncretism? Whatever it was, somehow

IN: INCARNATION & INCLUSION

Abba knew this seeker was calling. And when we call, who hears? Who answers? As a Christian, I would think it's the Lord who heard—and I would expect it was the Word who answered. We know that because the Voice was in sync with the Voice Paul heard when writing his epistle to the Romans. And now the Tai Chi guy knows too.

The Light came to him and it lingered with him and abided in him and spoke to him. Why didn't the Light identify as Jesus for thirty years? Wasn't *Abba* nervous about whether the man would die before hearing the Name? What if the Grace hadn't revealed Christ's Name prior to his death and the Final Judgment?

Fact: God only knows! *Abba* knew and was not anxious. Grace was playing the long game. For many of us, growing trust in the Light needs to predate the revelation of Jesus' Name because the Name has so often been associated more with Christless Christianity than with the true Light of the World.

Not that anyone would reject Jesus because Christians have misrepresented him ... Awkward!

Case in point: story #3

AMENDS

I was asked to represent "the organized church" for an addict who had to "make her amends."

In the world of addictions recovery, we "make amends" by working through an inventory of people or groups we have wronged or toward whom we hold resentments. We make our amends, not to secure forgiveness but to "own our sh*t." An analogy we use is that we're cleaning up our side of the road—no expectations are placed on the person we make our amends with.

As it happened, this woman admitted to me that she had judged "the church" (i.e., Christians) in general and confessed that she held them to standards she didn't live up to herself.

She brilliantly avoided retrying the church for its failures—for the hypocrisy of Christians who condemned her as less-than, who judged her and had done terrible things to instill fear in her as a child. She focused instead on ways some Christians had helped her family at various times.

I probed further because to truly rid ourselves of resentment, we can't minimize the ways we've been wronged. We must acknowledge the wrongs done and ultimately leave those offenses and our offenders with Christ.

I knew she had been in the program for a long time, so I asked her to describe the God she encountered through Christians. She said HE (with a capital H) was harsh and judgmental, to be feared and avoided—basically her projection of the abuse she had experienced. Then I asked her to describe the "Higher Power" she knew through 12-step recovery. As usual, she echoed the theology of their literature. Her Higher Power is loving, caring and forgiving. But there was more...

She had been through decades of addiction and all the spin-offs that entail. She'd overdosed numerous times and was brought back from death (or near death) by paramedics and doctors more than once.

IN: INCARNATION & INCLUSION

During an overdose episode ten years ago, she felt her life/spirit leaving her body. She knew she was dying. And then she said she saw a bright, white Light of pure Love. She reached out to the Light but instead of leaving this life to join the Light, the Light reached back and entered her life, broken as she was. It was exactly as Romans 5 says: while she was still ignorant of the gospel and alien to all things *Abba,* the Light of the cosmos loved her and by Grace, reconciled her to *Abba* —without even knowing God's name. I asked her where the pure Light now lives and she solemnly pointed to her heart.

"Of course it does," I said.

Over the past decade, even while her addiction continued to torment her, she would get down on her knees and pray for forty-five minutes every day. She came to know the Light and could recognize the Voice. Despite her negative experiences with Christian religion, she found fellowship with the true Light in her recovery meetings. In the Rooms, as addicts call them, the Light we describe as our Higher Power embraced her: loving her, caring for her, forgiving her and never coming across as "judgy."

For ten years, the Light did not reveal its Name until the day I met her. Oh, she'd heard of Jesus before, but never identified him with the Light. But when she was finally able to let go of her judgments and resentments toward the Church—we who had tarnished the Name—she could then hear my testimony:

"You said you've judged Christians without knowing what they believe. May I tell you?" She nodded and I continued, riffing off the prologue of John's Gospel:

Radical Encounters

"The true Light that made you and me and everything—the Light who saved you from death and lives in your heart—that Light came into the world. The Light's Voice (the Word) fully entered the human condition ('became flesh'). And that Light, that Voice, has a Name. If you want to see the true Light fully embodied in a human person, look at Jesus. Jesus showed us pure Love, especially in how he treated women. May I share two stories?"

For the first time in her life, she heard about how the true Light, enfleshed in Jesus as selfless Love, reached out to women just like her—broken women whom men had exploited, judged and excluded. I told her the story of the woman at the well and the woman caught in adultery. She learned how Jesus addressed their broken lives, not as moral failings but as the "acting out behaviors" of a deep spiritual thirst. She learned that the very Light she already knew in her heart—the Love that has been sating her cravings—is one and the same as the Name revealed in those stories.

Here is the logical progression she needs to work through:

1. The Light she called her "Higher Power" is loving, caring and forgiving.

2. Christianity had been unloving, uncaring and unforgiving in the Name of Jesus.

3. How then could she know Jesus is that Light?

She couldn't—not without first letting go of her resentments to her Christian offenders. This may explain why Jesus invested ten years of anonymity while not wasting a moment to fill her heart with Light and healing Grace.

She knows the Light—there's no question. Now she'll have to ponder what it means if Christ is that Light.

ABBA YOGA

I met a woman a while back who practices daily yoga. In fact, her dream is to become a registered yogini. Her yoga space includes a little shrine with, among other objects, a tiny Buddha statue and a 4"x4" framed painting of Jesus. She says she practices yoga, "not just to tighten my butt but to get my head out of it." That's her way of saying she's not just into yoga for the stretching and physical exercise, but to meditate for mental, emotional and spiritual health.

For her, yoga meditation is not merely an exercise in emptying the mind or the self. It's a form of prayer. She does yoga to let go of distractions and attachments and to practice the presence of God, pray to God and listen to God. She was not yet settled on which name best represents the God she hears.

"I've never had a good experience with church," she says. But she is keenly God-conscious—she knows God loves her and speaks to her. While meditating, she pictures herself sitting with God, leaning on his shoulder and just being loved. On multiple occasions, she's experienced God heal her of damaged emotions. Once, in meditation, she even felt Jesus (specifically) lay his hand on her and cure her of an ulcer..

She asks God to be part of her day and claims to feel him beside her when she goes out. That's when she feels inner peace. Apart from her attentiveness to the Presence of God, she finds serenity illusive. Life has dragged her through the

Radical Encounters

trials of childhood abuse, sexual assault, divorce, bankruptcy and an unsatisfying job. Her circumstances have been supremely difficult, but she is courageous—a survivor and overcomer. I'm convinced that she knows God, has met the Light and hears the Voice. Yes, she even knows the Name.

A lot of Christians are into yoga these days. They think they can strip it of its Hindu and Buddhist spirituality and go for the physical benefits. Many others are terrified of it because they don't think that distinction is so easily made. They worry about being demonized if they dabble in Eastern spirituality. Instead of inner peace, they suspect that yoga is an open door to spiritual bondage. It's a fair question.

That got me thinking: since yoga was deliberately developed as a method of prayer, intended to draw practitioners into deeper focus on whatever god they worship, why neglect its primary use? Why not use yoga to center our hearts and minds on the God we worship? In our case, the *Abba* of Jesus.

I'm not talking about syncretism—the forms of prayer we use are not the issue. The real key is the God we worship. We hold many other worship practices in common with the major world religions: prayer, hymns, bowing, kneeling, candles, etc. We don't abandon those practices just because other faiths use them too. If yoga was first a way to focus on prayer, couldn't those who practice yoga use it for prayers to *Abba*, rather than fleeing it or secularizing it?

Since this woman is already open to God and since she's even met Jesus in meditation, I made this suggestion:

"I know you don't identify as a Christian. But I know you're into yoga. And I know you want to become a yogini. Well, there are a lot of Christians who are also into yoga—or they'd like to be—but they're incredibly nervous around its eastern spirituality. But what if you started a yoga class for Christians (or whoever) and instead of using Buddhist or Hindu mantras, you called your approach *Abba* Yoga? Why not try to teach Christians how to meditate on the *Abba* that Jesus revealed?"

I shared my belief in Jesus' unique revelation of God as "Our *Abba*" and how he showed us through his life that our *Abba* is loving, caring and forgiving—one and the same Light she already meets in meditation. I talked about his call to surrender ourselves to his loving care and proposed an experiment:

"Next time you do yoga, why not try *Abba* as your mantra? In fact, why not try it right now? See what happens."

She seemed willing to give it a go. She closed her eyes and held her hands in the Gyan Mudra position (index fingers touching thumbs)—the classic yoga gesture for Wisdom (another of Christ's biblical names!).

"*Abba*," she said. Her face softened into peace. She took a breath and exhaled.

"*Abba*," she repeated. I detected a subtle surprised gasp.

"*Abba*," for the third time. How very Trinitarian. She let out a huge sigh, then opened her eyes wide with amazement.

"What happened?"

She said, "I've always felt God right beside me. But when I said, '*Abba*,' I felt him IN me! It was like my chest opened wide and my heart completely surrendered and I had total access! I feel him IN me! In my heart!"

Radical Encounters

I then followed up with, "What is he saying?"

She listened for a moment and said, "He says, *Follow me.*"

Here's the new dilemma. She doesn't believe in Jesus the same way I do. Yet through Jesus, she came to know and embrace and surrender to the name of *Abba*. I wonder if that counts. What do you think? Maybe Jesus showed her *Abba* so that *Abba* can further show her Jesus? This was a giant leap forward on her journey: she surrendered to *Abba,* experienced his indwelling presence and surrendered to him.

I have a feeling that she's going to help Christians encounter *Abba* in ways they've not yet experienced. After all, just as she knew the Light before knowing the Name, I know Christians who use Jesus' Name but seem not to know *Abba's* Light.

I admit I felt a little clever. But only until I found out *Abba* Yoga is already "a thing"! Christians all over the world have latched onto the same idea and use *Abba's* name as their mantra and focus. Go figure.

Having said all that, I don't do yoga. I'm not recruiting you to join a studio or buy yoga pants. I'm unafraid of yoga, other than the commitment it takes. I'm a slackard. I'm told there's an array of unhealthy approaches and spiritual dangers to yoga, including actual syncretism. I don't recommend that Christians opt for the mantras of other religions. My point is this: my would-be yogini friend met the Light and heard the Voice. Then through Jesus, she found greater access and deeper experience of *Abba* than she had known before. In other words, Christ is both the radically *inclusive* Light of the world and also our *unique* Way and total access to our *Abba*.

IN: INCARNATION & INCLUSION

"YOU'RE IN"

Dean, a friend and old college buddy of mine, has worked in the Canadian prison system as a chaplain, alongside other chaplains who range in faith from fundamentalist Christian pastors to Wiccan priestesses. Together, this team of diverse chaplains provides chapel services, general visitation and pastoral counseling. On the conservative end, Christian chaplains may emphasize guilt for one's sins and crimes, along with Christ's offer of forgiveness through repentance and faith.

Such an approach assumes that those who confess their sins and turn to Christ will be forgiven and included in his saving work. All well and good. Until, that is, these faithful servants discover that no one in prison is actually guilty of anything. Didn't you know? Every last one of them has been incarcerated by mistake. Someone else is to blame. A parent, a spouse, an employer or a lawyer—the "system screwed them over." Yes, they appreciate having chaplains to whom they can express their frustration. It's very cleansing to confess the sins of those who've failed them and with the system that oppresses them. But admission of guilt? ... don't hold your breath.

Yes, this is hyperbole—I'm exaggerating and generalizing—storytelling. But it's a story I've witnessed directly in my own forays into maximum and medium-security prison facilities.

So, from a classic Evangelical chaplain's point of view, apart from owning their crimes and until they sincerely repent of their sins, these lost inmates will remain outside and beyond the grace of God—unsaved.

That's one way to look at it.

Radical Encounters

But Dean began seeing things and people differently. Wanting to test his new perspective, he engaged in an extended and unsanctioned experiment. During conversations with the inmates, he began to casually and quietly drop in this phrase: "You're in."

"Pardon?"

"You're in."

"How do you mean?"

"This talk of God's love—of what Jesus did for us. You're in."

"But I'm not a Christian."

"That may be. I'm just saying, You're in."

And then the objections would flow.

"You don't know what I've done!"

And the confessions would commence.

"God can't love me like that."

"Why not?"

Admissions of guilt. Confessions of crimes.

Interesting. When the chaplains tried to convince inmates they were sinners, they were decidedly innocent. When Dean assured them they were forgiven and included in the love and grace of Christ, they self-disqualified.

"That may be," Dean said. "I'm just saying, you're in."

Inmates would hear, shake their heads and leave to ponder.

As months passed, Dean persevered in his experiment and persisted in his declaration: "You're in."

Even to his surprise, the kindness of God began to lead to repentance! Confronted with the radically inclusive Grace of *Abba,* stubbornness slipped into surrender, denials into confessions, and resistance into repentance. Chapel service attendance began to grow—doubling in short order. And the Evangelical chaplains were perplexed. How to explain the surge in "conversions," even by the traditional standards of "sinner's prayers" and baptisms.

Dean, what's your secret?

Apparently, Dean's secret is what Scriptures said all along: what Christ did, he did for all. All were included in his saving life, death and resurrection. All are "in" prior to faith and repentance—but declaring that truth ignites responses of faith and repentance. That's why we call faith a response to Christ's saving Grace, rather than a transaction that somehow purchases it. Yes, a response is necessary, but it's a response to to the good news, *Abba's* YES in Christ.

TIM HORTONS REVIVAL

True story: one night, at the invitation of a friend, I attended a revival meeting about thirty minutes from my home. On stage were a number of excited revivalists strutting around proclaiming the next "great move of God." They were waving silk banners and plastic swords, blowing shofars and prophesying revival fire.

I was dying inside—feeling cynical and judgmental. I turned to my friend Murray and said, "I need to get out of here. If this is revival, I'm not interested. This feels like hype—or spiritual masturbation—and it's all meaningless. If revival is going to happen, it has to happen in local coffee shops with real people or it's all meaningless."

Radical Encounters

Murray saw I was losing it and kindly invited me to take off with him to the Tim Hortons® coffee shop down the road. As we stood in line, Murray turned to me and said, "I hate it when God speaks to me in public."

"What do you mean?" I asked. He gestured to the woman behind the counter, an elderly Indian woman who was serving coffee and donuts. Her strong accent hinted that she was an immigrant. The only thing that struck me strange about her was that someone in her senior years should not need to work at a coffee shop so late at night. I checked the time; was it already 11 pm?

Murray said to me, "I think I'm supposed to pray for her. There's something wrong with her neck and shoulder."

I saw no evidence of that and shrugged.

Murray said, "Now that I told you, I guess I'm going to have to do it, eh?"

"Sure," I said. "Just let me order first."

Murray placed his order and then asked the woman, "Are you are suffering from pain in your neck and shoulders?"

The woman's eyes opened wide and she replied, "Oh yes, sir. I was in a very bad car accident. I injured my neck and I have pain all the way down my left side, my neck and shoulder and also my hip and leg. I cannot even drive a car because of it. My daughter must help me in and out of the car and needs to drop me off and pick me up after every shift. These shifts are very late and standing for so long is very painful."

"May I pray for you?" Murray asked.

The woman looked confused but nodded, "I suppose so,"

not really knowing what to expect.

Murray gently extended his hand toward her (without touching her) and prayed a simple prayer. "Lord Jesus, I know you love this woman. Would you please heal her injury and remove her pain?"

Her eyes welled up with tears and Murray asked, "Do you feel any difference?" The woman carefully turned her head, testing her range of motion and said tentatively, "Yes, sir. I think it feels a little looser."

Murray prayed again, "Lord, thank you for your healing. I ask you to complete it. Amen."

Emboldened by Murray's faith, it was my turn. In faith, I made my requests known: "And I will have a medium coffee, one cream, and a cinnamon raisin bagel-regular cream cheese, please."

Murray and I sat down and debriefed the evening. I told him how completely done I was with revival meetings. I told him I never wanted to attend one again. I reiterated my earlier comment: if Christ doesn't "show up" here, touching normal people like this injured, elderly immigrant woman, what's the point of a jacked-up revival meeting?

As we continued chatting, we realized the Indian woman was now mopping the floor around our table—repeatedly. When we acknowledged her presence, she smiled at us, radiant with joy. She also seemed completely mobile. She was practically waltzing with the mop, swishing it around dramatically. After several revolutions around our section, Murray asked her, "How are you feeling?"

Radical Encounters

She blurted out with glee, "I couldn't do this before!" and began hopping up-and-down like the lame man healed in Acts chapter 3!

Murray said, "That's wonderful! Jesus has healed you!"

The woman said, "Well, I believe anyone who sincerely prays to God—no matter what name we use—God hears them, and will answer their prayer."

Murray smiled and said, "Well, I know God loves you. And he heard our prayers. I'm just saying, that was Jesus who healed you."

The woman replied, "Do you think God sent you here so that I would know Jesus healed me?"

"Could be, could be."

Moral of the story: The mustard seed kingdom is not about stadiums and fireworks. It grows quietly but powerfully, one coffee at a time, one immigrant at a time, one prayer at a time, one healing at a time. It's *Abba's* dream for this world. The real world. Your world. Not someday, but this day and in a coffee shop in your town.

"RAYMOND, YOU KNOW MY NAME"

Ray Loewen is a friend from Altona, Canada. He first shared this story in my book, *Kissing the Leper*. In his own words:

On a frigid evening in February 2001, ten people from Altona, MB, Canada drove into the city of Winnipeg to participate in an evening of praise and worship at the Vineyard Church. The church was located just off Main Street, an area often busy with glue-sniffers, prostitutes, and the poorest folks in the city. We parked our cars in front of the church and gathered inside for an incredible time of worship.

After the service, while returning to our cars, we noticed a couple coming down the street. She kept walking, not really paying attention to us. But the mangy looking man stopped and began to plead for some money.

"Hey, buddy. Got any change? I need some money," he slurred. Some in our group, perhaps nervous, made for their cars, but I moved toward him, fumbling in my jacket pockets for change. As I got closer, I was greeted by the overpowering smell of alcohol and glue on his breath. In the icy weather, he had drooled over his scraggly beard, which was now matted and frozen over with saliva icicles. He kept pressing, now more insistent,

"Hurry up, she's getting away," referring to his companion who was disappearing down the street.

I still remember fumbling for change and making excuses about not having much money to give...

At that point, he looked directly at me and said in a clear, firm voice: "You know me, *Raymond*. Hurry up and give me some money."

As you can imagine, the rational side of my brain went a little nuts. I was hit by a barrage of thoughts: "Why did you call me *Raymond*? Nobody has called me that since I was a kid. And I always hated that name. What do you mean you know me? I don't know you! We've never met! You can't know me!"

Okay, this was just a coincidence. He picked a name, and it just so happens that of the two hundred people leaving the church, he picked mine! He must have meant that *his* name was Raymond.

I thought he must have been trying to say, "You know me.

Radical Encounters

I'm Raymond."

Again, just a coincidence? We just happened to share the same name and be the two people who would face off on a cold winter night in the north end of Winnipeg?

While the analytical side of my brain was screaming along at warp speed trying in vain to rationalize what had just happened, my intuitive side began to recall Jesus' words in the Gospel of Matthew where he describes the judgment of the sheep and goats. I could see the story in my mind's eye even while the man held out his hand.

Eugene Peterson's *The Message* tells the story of Matthew 25 this way:

> When he finally arrives, blazing in beauty and all his angels with him, the Son of Man will take his place on his glorious throne. Then all the nations will be arranged before him and he will sort the people out, much as a shepherd sorts out sheep and goats, putting sheep to his right and goats to his left ... then he will turn to the goats, the ones on his left, and say,
>
> "Get out worthless goats. You're good for nothing but the fires of hell. And why? Because: I was hungry and you gave me no meal. I was thirsty and you gave me no drink. I was homeless and you gave me no bed. I was shivering and you gave me no clothes. Sick and in prison, and you never visited."
>
> Then those goats are going to say, "Master what are you talking about? When did we see you hungry, shivering or sick or in prison and didn't help?"
>
> He will answer them, "I'm telling the solemn truth—whenever you failed to do one of these things to someone

who was being overlooked or ignored, that was me—you failed to do it to me."

That night on the cold streets of Winnipeg, I saw myself standing before God's judgment throne and hearing Jesus say,
"Remember that night just off Main Street? I even called you by name, and still you ignored me..."
"You know me, Raymond."

In that epiphany, I discovered God's purpose for me. By day, I sell used cars in Southern Manitoba. But God's purpose in me had a lot more to do with Jesus' challenge to meet him on the road in the least and the lost—and a lot less to do with getting more consumers on the road in cars and trucks.

RAYMOND VISITS EL SALVADOR (THE SAVIOR)

Several months later, on September 2001, I made my first trip to El Salvador as part of the Mennonite Central Committee's (MCC) *Build a Village* project, which involves raising money and building homes for earthquake victims. By then, I had helped prepare two other "work and learn" teams but had never gone myself. My plan was to go to El Salvador and live out Matthew 25. I was going to help someone in need, to provide a home for a family that did not have one. Two days after arriving in the country, I became sick, first with an upset stomach from the food or the water, then on the second evening, with a severe pain in my back which I had never experienced before (which turned out to be a kidney stone attack).

I was lying on a mat on the cement floor of the community center feeling miserable and a little sorry for myself. I was

Radical Encounters

asking God some "Why?" questions, as in "Why me?" and "Why now?"

After all, he knew how I had longed to come to El Salvador to live out his words from Matthew 25. Couldn't we arrange for this pain to come back in a few weeks after my return to Canada? Everything was backwards. Others were bringing me food and drink, visiting me when I was sick, coming to pray with me for healing! People were coming to care for me and feed me and love me!

On the second morning, it hit me: I was living out the verses in Matthew 25! But I had expected to live them as the "giver."

Now I was experiencing them as the "receiver." I had never expected to learn it this way, but God used my illness to confirm the importance of the Matthew 25 kind of compassion:

> Then the King will say to those on his right, "Enter, you who are blessed by my Father! Take what's coming to you in this kingdom. It's been ready for you since the world's foundation. And here's why: I was hungry and you fed me, I was thirsty and you gave me a drink, I was homeless and you gave me a room, I was shivering and you gave me clothes, I was sick and you stopped to visit, I was in prison and you came to me."
>
> Then those 'sheep' are going to say,
>
> "Master, what are you talking about? When did we ever see you hungry and feed you, thirsty and give you a drink? And when did we ever see you sick or in prison and come to you?"
>
> Then the King will say, "I'm telling the solemn truth: Whenever you did one of these things to someone over-

looked or ignored, that was me—you did it to me."
—Matthew 25:34-40 (MSG)

Thanks, Raymond. Yes, the *Jesus Way* does call for *radical compassion* for those of every type of poverty—to follow Christ in *radical identification* for the visible or invisible suffering in all its forms. The gospel was, from its inception, a call to take up the cross of co-suffering love. Self-giving love stands at the heart of the gospel. It's not an option, an appendix, addendum or a footnote.

THOUGHTS

1. Does the Apostle Peter's generous assessment of Cornelius' pre-Christian spirituality strike you as an open door for syncretism? How does practicing yoga or Tai Chi go a step further, given their Hindu or Buddhist roots? Do you think replanting these practices in Christian soil is sufficient? Is it sufficient to redirect these practices toward *Abba*? Is *Abba's* appearance in these practices intended as an endorsement of them, irrelevant to them, or a rescue from them? Are they preferred, optional or forbidden ways of worshiping Christ?

2. What do you make of Dean's assurance to the prisoners he visits: "You're in!"? Which New Testament texts affirm that all are in Christ via the Incarnation? Which biblical texts support the unique "in-ness" of Christ-followers? How would you distinguish these? How is the spatial metaphor of "in-out" language helpful or unhelpful?

Radical Encounters

PRAYERS

Lord Jesus Christ, I thank you that you did not simply wait for us to come find you on the Jesus Way. Grace came looking for us on a multitude of paths that were leading nowhere. Our Good Shepherd entered pits we had dug for ourselves and rescued us when escape was hopeless. Our Abba ran to us when we were still a long way off. We've too often looked for your approval of our own ways—but now that we've met you, we ask you to lead us into your Way.

RADICAL RELEASE
The Priest at Jesus' Feet

> "DO YOU COMMIT SIN? Enter the church and repent of your sin; for here is the Physician, not the judge; here one is not investigated, one receives remission of sins."
>
> —St. John Chrysostom

THE F-WORD

In 2009, I experienced the sacred privilege of participating in a healing circle with First Nations people who had only sort of survived unspeakable abuse in Canada's infamous residential schools (mostly run as Anglican or Catholic institutions). I heard the sordid stories and witnessed the harmful impact of religious-political dehumanization of these tender souls, even decades after the fact. I learned how some still live in the hell of permanent consequences to their lives and families. In some cases, freedom only came through a painful process of truth-telling, forgiveness and reconciliation. But for others, "forgiveness" is the F-word used to justify the abuse, demand their silence and compel them to repress their stories as emotional tumors. Forgiveness to them was just another religious demand—a nail in the coffin of their personhood.

For that reason, it's essential that I begin this chapter on radical forgiveness with a primary on what forgiveness is not lest those who read it mishear me. The forgiveness of Christ is radical and scandalous and probably the most difficult element of the Jesus Way. We certainly don't want an abusive, false forgiveness to make the Way impossible or to divert it from us altogether. Our healing and freedom are too important to allow it to be sabotaged by the F-word.

WHAT FORGIVENESS IS NOT

Forgiveness is NOT saying, "It's okay." The sin of harming *Abba's* dear children is NOT okay. Abuse and oppression are never acceptable. Forgiveness must not minimize injustice or the damage it does.

Forgiveness is NOT saying, "I'm okay." Healing can take years. Genuine forgiveness does not ask anyone to skip any stage of the grieving and healing process.

Forgiveness is NOT saying, "You're okay." The offender is not simply off the hook. Repentance includes facing consequences, which may include incarceration, rehabilitation, restitution and restoration.

Forgiveness is NOT saying, "We're okay." Forgiveness may include but does not require the victim of injustice to re-enter a relationship with the offender. That may not be possible or even safe. One can forgive and be healed without ever being reconciled to the offender.

FORGIVENESS MEANS LETTING GO

Then what does genuine forgiveness look like? Forgiveness literally means "let go," loose or release. This release includes at least six specific layers that I prefer to do at the Cross of Christ.

1. Forgiveness happens when we release our offenders to Christ's judgment, rather than chaining our hearts to them with resentment. We tend to become like those we resent but become free from those we forgive. So, we allow Christ to unbind us from them and trust *Abba* to heal one and all by his love and mercy. This doesn't mean we bypass human justice systems when necessary. But it means our healing doesn't depend on human courts getting it right.

2. Forgiveness happens when we release our burdens of hurt, grief, anger, loss and sorrow to *Abba's* care, rather than stuffing them or fashioning them into weapons. We exchange them for the Creator's love, joy, peace and healing mercy. We look to God, rather than our own outrage and indignation, for strength and wisdom to fight ongoing battles, lest we perpetuate injustice in our own families and communities.

3. Forgiveness happens when we release the debt of the other's offense into God's hands. Even if they repent sincerely and make restitution, our offenders can never cover the debt of harms done. We must let God bear that burden—ours and theirs. For Christians, the Cross is our most powerful image of this divine "sin-bearing."

4. Forgiveness happens when we release our healing into God's hands. No one's punishment or repentance is sufficient to heal us. Only God can truly do that. Our healing is NOT in the hands of the ones who hurt us. Surrendering to God's care within a community of reconciliation makes healing possible.

Radical Release

5. Forgiveness happens when we release our guilt into God's hands. Many former residents of St. George's residential school saw how their experience there shaped them into abusers, addicts and criminals. When they finally owned their own wrongs and gave their own guilt to God, healing became possible.

6. Forgiveness happens when, having let go, we surrender our lives to Christ's love and care. One man shared the story of how his pain had led him into years of addiction, homelessness and alienation from family and community. In his pain, he had damaged everyone in his life and was ready to take his own life. But God and his community walked him beyond shame and humiliation to receive forgiveness and belonging. His community became the welcoming arms of the Creator, agents of his restoration and reconciliation.

By clarifying what forgiveness is and what it is not, we're prepared for a deeper look at how radical and scandalous the real deal can be.

7. Forgiveness is nothing less than the central theme of the Cross of Christ and we dare to say that there is absolutely nothing his blood can't wash.

THE PRIEST AT JESUS' FEET

A woman crouches at Jesus' feet, caught red-handed in the act of adultery and on the brink of temple-sponsored capital punishment. Then in an act of courage and brilliance, Jesus saves her from her accusers! Such scandalous grace!

But do we really think so?

IN: INCARNATION & INCLUSION

How we've sanitized the scandal by romanticizing the adulteress, perhaps imagining a pretty woman—say, Julia Roberts—instead of the $20 "crack-whore," her face asymmetrical from beatings inflicted by pimps and johns who traffic and devour them.

How we (male readers) promote our egos by casting ourselves into the scene as pure and clever and gutsy—a Jesus/Richard Gere hybrid swaggering in for the rescue. Or at best, we're the woman, grateful for a Savior at the eleventh hour. But often, we're so out of touch with scandalous grace that we don't readily identify with the stone-tossing Pharisee or the creepy john repressed within us by our paper-thin moralism. What about the furious jilted wife and confused children of the unfaithful man? And hang on—where is he anyway?

No, our version of John 8 is typically not scandalous. It's too often been sugar-coated into a sweet Prince Charming and Cinderella story.

Today, ministry front-liners who rescue victims of sex-trafficking are seen as the most Christlike activists out there. The kudos they get are well-deserved, the donations they're sent are well-invested. These are good people—my favorites, truly. I commend their work as worthwhile and noble. But unlike Christ (and because of Christ), their intervention is viewed as heroic rather than scandalous. That's a good thing. It's just that we now miss the messy edge of how far cruciform forgiveness extends.

Radical Release

MAKE JESUS SCANDALOUS AGAIN

Try this on for a slogan: *Make Jesus Scandalous Again.* What if the pathetic sinner at Jesus' feet is unforgivable? What if it's a serial pedophile caught [finally!] in the act? What if he's a priest or one of the infamous Cardinals responsible for covering up crimes against children?

And what if the mob bearing stones are not religious conspirators in the Temple establishment but real victims of his institution's chronic clergy abuses, finally empowered to speak their truth? What if they're activists who, through social media, now have enough social traction to take down the perpetrator and the whole God-damned infrastructure.

Now, at last, WWJD? gets interesting.

Maybe Jesus takes a giant step back and says, "Have at it, boys and girls—it's time for a good purge. Vengeance is yours this time! Enjoy!"

Would he have picked up his own stone? I can imagine the agitated crowd squirming a little in that case too—suspicious of Jesus' motives and anxious about his next move.

Maybe Jesus puts on his Crocodile Dundee accent and sneers, "Those aren't stones. This is a stone!" as he materializes a millstone from beneath his tunic. Would Christ commence to tie it around sinner-man's neck and say, "Better had you never been born"?

And fair enough, right? He says so directly in Matthew 18:6.

Of course, we might balk at this version of the story.

For one, the woman was not the perpetrator, was she? We

know from the text that she was a pawn in a set-up, the victim of religious subterfuge. I like to see her as the innocent victim of patriarchal manipulation. I'm 100% sure she was.

But the john's wife and children might disagree. To them, she was more likely the seductress, the homewrecker, "the bitch who stole my husband/dad."

We might also object that the priest is an unrepentant serial offender. But wait. Was this merely a one-off for the ensnared woman? And where does the passage say the woman repented? I don't read that anywhere in John 8. The story never minimizes her guilt—our doing so only minimizes the scandal and scope of Christ's radical forgiveness.

I read that she was caught in adultery. That she was dragged in for execution under the Law.

She was saved by Grace alone—not by innocence, not by repentance, not by faith. This was a gratuitous rescue completely independent of her guilt or innocence, her choices or any response to Christ whatsoever.

And anyway, would it matter? Is that how the gospel works?

Did Jesus die only for innocent victims?

Did he come only for repentant sinners?

Is Christ's blood sufficient for the exploited, but not enough for the perpetrator?

These are the days when Romans 5 needs reviewing again and again. When we were weak, Christ died for us. When we were sinners, Christ forgave us. When we were unrepentant enemies, Christ reconciled us to God. Grace first, always. The key to the woman's salvation was Christ's identification and

Radical Release

solidarity with her. The plot, if I understand it, was to stone them both—her for adultery and him for "leading Israel astray" (Deut. 13). Double or nothing.

DIVINE SOLIDARITY

My friend, Kenneth Tanner, put it this way:

> Divine solidarity with humanity is radical. Jesus is not only in the corner of humanity but in every human's corner *as* a fellow human who also happens to be God ... There is no human with whom Jesus does not stand. Not one person. Not one! Against every hurled accusation, every derision, and all that mocks our existence: famine, decay, murder, disaster, disease, and death, Jesus has our back. Always.
>
> Jesus stands with humanity and with *every* human person ... against all that accuses us and belittles us and seeks to destroy us, and he does this as our human brother and as God.

That sounds beautiful and inspiring and wonderful. I wish I had said it. But then I stumble. I remember the priests and pedophiles. Forgiveness is not just radical. Forgiveness of the perp is the scandalous and nauseating f-word.

And then I remember myself. Who am I? The sinner at Jesus' feet or the holy man bearing stones? What'll it be, Brad? Mercy or condemnation?

My inclination to mercy comes not because I think I'm morally superior to those wicked men, whether that's the stone-bearing conspirators or the corrupt priests who've harmed countless kids. And yes, both are undeniably and deliberately wicked. Rather, I choose mercy and forgiveness because I see the darkness that lurks in me. I cringe remembering the ways I've harmed others through the years. My own disqualifying guilt leaves me without a leg of self-righteous outrage on which to stand. I'm inclined to mercy because that's what I need. And I'm obligated to mercy because that's what I've received from *Abba* and through the very people I hurt most.

Those who could have condemned me not only dropped their stones, but dropped to their knees with me in the dust and scribbled *Abba's* Grace in my dirt. Instead of saying, "Rot in hell, you bastard," they echoed Christ: "Neither do I condemn you; go and sin no more," knowing I probably will. And there, the beauty and scandal of forgiveness come together.

All I know is, I don't get to stand in the land of Grace and restoration while I condemn someone else to the land of the law and retribution. The measure with which I judge, I will be judged. Jesus said that. I don't get to demand the hammer for others and expect the feather for myself.

What then? I pray for the victims of the clergy's many sins, mine included. I pray for the mercy of such deep-level healing that their cry for justice will transcend retribution and bring the true justice of a redeemed world.

For the perpetrators, I pray for the severe mercy of rigorous honesty, heart-rending repentance, appropriate penance and real freedom to become more than what they are now.

Radical Release

For myself, I pray, "Lord Jesus Christ, Son of God, have mercy on me, a sinner" and "God, grant them the same mercy I want for myself."

By God's Grace, I have had the great privilege of a front-row seat to witness Christ heal the most broken, forgive the 'unforgivable' and redeem the most perverse by his transforming mercy.

DAVID'S CONFESSION

I first met David (an alias) at a men's retreat in Tennessee.

Picture this: one hundred Jesus-loving Southern gentlemen packed into a galvanized steel workshed, decorated with stuffed wildlife trophies, antique license plates and a string of Christmas lights fashioned from used shotgun shells. Our teaching times expressed gratitude for God's bottomless spring of amazing love. Between downpours and hailstorms, the weather was insanely muggy but it wasn't all just sweaty rednecks singing "Kumbaya." We were swimming in a magnificent flow of grace, tears and beers.

Sure, beers ... if Miller Lite qualifies. I'm skeptical, but even so, I was grateful that our host stocked iceboxes on such hot, humid days. Some believe the Trinity and alcohol don't mix—certainly not with American lite beer. Nevertheless, the men behaved, and the conversation focused on the Father, Son and Holy Spirit and our inclusion in the divine dance of triune love. Though I am typically leery of all-male gatherings, I saw men open up who would never dare in mixed company. The fellowship was raw and real, and so were those tears.

I didn't launch a poll of how many men were "packing,"

but not a few hinted at their NRA affiliation and concealed carry permits. One fellow, a jovial friend who lives to serve the needs of children, confided in me that he would surely use his sidearm if he ever met a pedophile. With conviction, he insisted that such "animals" need to be "put down." You see, like you, he loves kids and finds it unthinkable that anyone should ever injure one of these little ones. Remember Jesus' warning: better they should be collared with a millstone and dumped overboard at sea. I get it. If there is a worst sin, molesting children ranks at the top. We're all about grace, but it's not really "unconditional," is it? I mean, come on!

During a break, a man I'll call David asked to speak with me privately. He and his friend led me out to the wild-grass out of earshot from the other men. Trembling, David began his confession. He told me about how, years earlier, he had molested his own daughter. Then, when he began grooming his second daughter likewise, the older teen would not have it. She fought through her fears to bring what her father had done to light and to justice.

David was charged, convicted and sentenced to prison. Graciously, his friend had supported him with visits, letters, phone calls, money and books throughout the full term of his incarceration. And while David had supposedly "paid his debt to society," prison time did nothing to heal his daughters or to address the roots of David's sickness, sins and crimes. His sentence was strictly retributive—David was punished by the state, by his conscience, and by all that happens to sex offenders of his type in prison.

Radical Release

At that point in his story, David looked me in the eyes and said, "Jesus was right. I promise you: it would have been better for me to have a large millstone hung around my neck and to be drowned at sea." He knew by direct experience that such swift justice would have been, for him, an act of mercy.

But here he was, free at last but not yet free at all. Now on the Georgian sex offenders' registry, he was only permitted to attend our gathering by warning the organizers of his history, securing their permission to come, and traveling with a companion—this friend who stuck closer than a brother.

Now he was asking for healing.

If all our talk of radical grace and forgiveness does not apply to him—if Jesus' blood can wash anything and anyone, except for David—then he's done for. And so am I. And so are you.

In prayer, I asked Jesus to take us to the very roots of his sexual brokenness. David began to sob immediately. He recounted how he had stumbled into habitual masturbation when he was five years old. When his stepfather caught him "sinning," little Davie was dragged out to the barn and beaten. His stepdad tied him to a chair and lashed him with a leather strap—repeatedly, mercilessly. That first time, little Davie felt all the physical pain of the whipping and the emotional pain of his stepfather's belittling words and hateful rejection. He wasn't merely being punished—he was literally being tortured and emasculated.

After that, little Davie endured many more such trips to the barn. After the first incident, our Lord Jesus—himself acquainted with the cruelty of the whip—granted the gift of dissociation. David remembers his spirit hovering outside, floating above the barn roof and listening to himself scream, yet no longer feeling the physical pain.

I asked Jesus to enter that terrible memory and to rescue little David from his stepdad, from the endless whipping, from the ropes that held him and from the pain of his childhood torment. As David continued to watch the scene in his memory, he recounted the following, in his own words:

> Jesus entered the barn and found the little boy. He untied the bonds. And then, with "little Davie" in the middle, Jesus stood on his left and I [adult David] stood on his right. We put our arms around little Davie and together, watched the barn roof dissolve into a sheet and ascend.
>
> Then Jesus took me to a lake. I saw him squatting at the base of the tree, wearing overalls and a plaid shirt. And he was twirling a flower—a lily—which had yet to bloom. I just knew he wanted to hear me, to listen to me.

David wept gently in the presence of Jesus until the moment passed. We sat quietly in the grass, catching our breath. The whole process had taken just twenty minutes, but decades of trauma had lifted. Over a year later, he can testify that while his healing is still unfolding, that particular memory has been completely healed. It is no longer a storehouse for fear and torment—the barn in his heart is gone. As a result, he's become free enough to begin the hard work of making amends with his family. He puts no demands on them for

Radical Release

forgiveness, but he is seeing profound movement toward reconciliation.

But there was also immediate fruit from our visit to the barn with Jesus. When it came time for the final sharing session as a group, David felt stirred to share his experience with the men. Maybe the residual adrenaline from his healing encounter was still pumping.

"Yikes," I thought, "confess to these guys? Would that be safe?" I made sure my new friend didn't feel obligated to tell his story from the stage. But he assured me it's what he wanted. And I assured him that I'd stand with him as he shared.

When his moment came, David and I stood before the men and I paraphrased the verse from Hebrews 2:11 that says, "For the one who makes others holy, and the ones who are made holy, all belong to a single family. This is why he isn't ashamed to call them his brothers and sisters."

I told the men that David had something to say and that I was not ashamed to call him my brother. I put my arm around him and held the microphone for him. He buried his face in my shoulder and began to weep again. Still, he soldiered on and spoke out all that I've said above. For my part, I felt Christ-in-me, taking his firm stand beside David and watching the crowd with confidence and perhaps vigilance?

I must say, the scene before me was darkly comical. The men were completely gob-smacked—their jaws hung open and eyes were all a-bulge like Hannah-Barbara cartoon characters! They were awe-struck by the abuse David had undergone, the crimes he had committed and the grace of God in his retroactive healing. They were so arrested by the emotional conundrum and by the kindness of Jesus that vigilante fantasies fled their minds. In view of Christ's radical forgiveness, any would-be stone-throwers were disarmed by mercy.

David recalls an audible gasp from someone in the crowd, first, when he confessed that his daughters were his victims, and again when he shared his revelation of Jesus saving him from the barn. The urge to run was strong, but God gave him the courage to continue.

THE CALL

One day my cell phone rang. I didn't recognize the number on call-display. Normally, I wouldn't pick up, but today I felt a strong inner nudge to answer.

"Hello?"

A man was bawling on the other end. He couldn't speak or identify himself, but I knew in my heart it was David.

"Take your time," I said. "I'm here."

Eventually, he blurted out, "I don't know what happened! I didn't know who else to call!" And then back to weeping.

I waited anxiously, wondering if David had somehow dissociated again and had a relapse. If he had, isn't that exactly what he would say?

Again, "Take your time."

Finally, he managed to explain that he'd tried calling his best friend but couldn't get through. "I didn't know who else to call," he repeated.

Radical Release

"It's good, David. You were meant to call me. What's happened?"

"I was on my way to my mother's house. I was driving and one road led to another ... I can't explain how it happened. But I drove by our old property. And now I'm at my mom's in the driveway and I don't know what to do."

Again, "What happened, David?"

"It's the Barn! The Barn is gone!"

"What do you mean, it's gone?"

"The actual barn! Someone tore it down! It's gone!"

The Barn is gone! At long last, thank God, the Barn is gone!

JACKI'S CONFESSION

The reason David's story of forgiveness is so radical is because the worst sins we can imagine involve harming children. That's one reason why the abortion wars continue to rage. Another reason is our paralysis of polarized strategies on how best to address abortion faithfully.

The following confession is not about that debate. It's about radical forgiveness in the extreme. What I'll describe is an experience—not a political position, not a theology, not an ontology, not a solution. I don't even know how to assess it. I'm just the reporter here. I literally just copied and pasted the following from an extended text string.

Jacki (her real name) is a friend who was abused (molested, raped, beaten) frequently (often daily) from infancy until she left home. The perpetrators included her father, relatives, clergy and others. Among the ongoing symptoms of her abuse, she suffers from dissociative identity disorder, painful and irreversible scarring in her reproductive tract from hundreds of childhood rapes, regular seizures, a four-decade struggle with drug addiction and recurring suicidal ideations.

It was our great privilege to meet years ago for "listening prayer" ministry in Della Headley's office. We have maintained our friendship to this day. Through her trials and ongoing pain, we learned how to meet, behold and listen to Jesus.

That was no magic fix. She's still had to fight for her life for years. The following conversation occurred over the course of a weekend and marks a landmark in her recovery. I share the following healing experience with her permission.

Activating event: Jacki had seen a graphic and gruesome description of how late-term abortion works on social media. It was an excerpt from a condemning report that someone posted to cause outrage and shame. It described her actions as unforgivable.

It nearly cost Jacki her life.

You see, on two occasions, her dad had impregnated her via rape. Unable to accept that reality, she hid her pregnancy for as long as possible. When hiding the truth became impossible, she terminated both pregnancies.

Yes, she desperately aborted two of her father's children. The article brought it all back and described in vivid detail what she had done.

Did it?

Did she?

She contacted me in a panic:

Radical Release

Jacki: "I read this today and I gasped when I read it!" She forwarded me a screenshot of the article. "Brad, I did this with my dad's babies. I did it because I waited and hid my pregnancy because I couldn't accept it. How do I live with myself? I can't EVER forgive myself. NEVER! I feel like my life is over. I can't live with this! I can't.

I should have had those babies somewhere and given them away ... or aborted them before they would have suffered. I dealt with the abortions with Jesus ... but I didn't know I had done THIS!

I'm accountable for what I did to innocent babies! Like WTF? Isn't this the worst thing in the world?!

Brad: No. Being put in that impossible position might be. Literally impossible. You don't have the divine wisdom to know what you should have done or the divine power to change what is done or the divine right to hold yourself in a court or prison that doesn't belong to you.

What you can do is send yourself to Jesus for his judgment and wait for his verdict. I'm very firm on this: playing the part of your own unmerciful god is a dangerous and unholy path. Let yourself go to him.

Jacki: I treated the most innocent creations in the world like they were nothing. I caused them writhing pain and suffering. I did that! I did that. I did that.

Brad: They are at complete peace in Jesus' arms now. What do you think they want of you now? Would they have you abandon your living family and little grandchildren as some kind of retribution? These children only know grace.

You need to look Jesus in the eyes on this one.

Jacki: I'm too ashamed. And they didn't always know peace. They knew great pain—from ME!

Brad: You only have two options: follow shame away from Jesus or look to Jesus to wash your shame. I hope you make the choice that leads to freedom.

Jacki: I deserve to sit in the shame forever for what I did. I should be locked up for the gruesome murder of two lives!

Sometimes we have to pay for our sins. I choose the pain! Forever!

Brad: It won't end well.

Jacki: No, it won't.

Brad: Jacki, Christ's verdict is always mercy. But retracting your surrender can be fatal.

Jacki: Maybe I want that ... to die so I will have to face his judgment.

You tell me, Brad. What do you feel about me now? Knowing what you know of what I did? The evil I am capable of? All I hear in my head is the screams of babies in excruciating pain. You tell me how to make up for what I did?

Brad: You don't make up for it. You can't. No punishment or payment solves any sin, no matter how small or big. There is only Jesus' blood that absorbs it in Grace.

Your penance is worthless because it doesn't work.

Your attempts to make it right got you here in the first

Radical Release

place. Abortion didn't wash away your shame.

But Jesus already has. Picking up this obsession again made you forget that.

How do I feel about your abortion? Complete forgiveness because Jesus already forgave you. He's the only one with the right to judge, and he already made his judgment.

How do I feel about your refusal to turn to him now? Honestly? Sad. Sad to see you reject someone who has shown you nothing but kindness. The obsession gives you amnesia. But willfulness goes like that.

Your choice.

Jacki: I'd never done anything so absolutely disgusting before. My head is a revolving door right now.

Brad: Go to Jesus.

Jacki: Please don't be mad at me.

Brad: Go to Jesus.

Jacki: Okay, I'll go.

Brad: Great! Let me know the whole story. Go to him and stay until he's completely done, okay?

AT JESUS' FEET

Jacki: I went to Jesus and I literally fell to my knees and sobbed. I couldn't look at him.

He put his hand on the back of my head as I crouched on the floor at his feet. He said, "Look at my eyes."

I said, "I can't. I did the worst thing someone could ever do."

He said, "Look up. I have something to show you."

IN: INCARNATION & INCLUSION

I finally looked up and there on Jesus' lap sat two little girls who were about two-years-old. They were dressed in different colors, but their dresses were the same: baby pink and lavender. They looked like me at that age only way more beautiful. And their eyes shone with joy and peace! Jesus told me their names were Joy and Love.

I asked, "Is that them?"

He said, "Yes. They grew but never passed two. They seem to like to be this age. They are always together. Always. They don't know pain and never have."

I cried and cried and said, "How is that possible after what I did to them? After what I did? I hurt them and killed them."

He said, "You didn't kill them. I saved them! Before they felt pain, I took them from your womb, and they have been with me ever since."

I said, "But I chose to kill them."

He said, "You were in the most painful time of your life. You didn't choose to kill them. I chose to take them."

He said, "I knew one day you would find this out and we would have to talk. I always knew you would come to me, no matter how ashamed you were. I know you love me, and I am the Savior of your soul."

He said, "I want you to love yourself. You are too hard on yourself. You forget what suffering you were living every day. I'm pleased you came to me. You don't ever have to be afraid to come to me. Now come and meet our precious little ones."

So I touched their little hands and kissed their cheeks. Then they ran away carefree with some angels.

Radical Release

Jesus said, "Come to me. Climb up on my lap and let me love you. Cry on my robe. I will heal your broken heart. I am sorry for what you went through. I know. And I always loved you. Every single day. Cry now... but don't cry for the babies... or from shame... cry as you forgive yourself. And I will help you see your true beautiful, loving heart. I am proud of you. And I love you always. And when you are done crying—you will see it over time—that all is well. You will be able to feel it and accept it. And the hatred you feel for yourself will drift away. My gift to you is this: anytime you want to see any of your babies, you can come to me and we will play together. All you have to do is ask."

I sobbed, "Thank you, my Jesus. Thank you, my Jesus."

Unforgivable? For Jesus?

Maybe we need to stop asking (with Paul's opponents), "What? Shall we continue to sin that grace may abound?" and ask ourselves, "What? Shall we continue to condemn so that shame may abound?" May it never be!

"THAT WAS TOO EASY"

One reason forgiveness becomes the f-word is that we mistake it for a cheap "Get out of jail free" card. Absolution sounds too easy.

But no. No, it's not. Not for me and especially not for Jesus.

Josh (not his real name) was a tender man—I don't recall ever having a conversation with him in which he didn't weep. I eventually discovered he was a broken man—a sex addict who couldn't hold a relationship together. He finally disclosed that as a teen, he had taken advantage of children he had once babysat. The family found out but for whatever reason, possibly because he had been quite young, Josh had been released without punishment. But that wasn't quite true. He lived with the crushing burden of daily guilt and being a relational cripple. Forgiving himself was a bridge too far.

As for me, I had been praying with victims for years, but this was my first exposure—my trial by fire—to working with a perpetrator. My resentment showed. All I could think to do was take him to Jesus by the scruff of the neck. I directed Josh to close his eyes and stand before the Cross. Normally, I would suggest picturing the resurrected standing before the cross, arms open in invitation. This time I said, "Josh, I want you to open the eyes of your heart to see Christ hanging on the Cross. Can you do that?"

He merely nodded and began blubbering.

I was curt: "Tell him what you did."

Josh babbled through a full confession. When he finished, I said, "Now look Jesus in the face. What does he say to you?"

"He says, 'I forgive you!'"

I didn't quite know what to say. It seemed like the right words, but it seemed too easy. It seemed like we had missed something. Before I could sort out how to proceed, Josh said it for me.

"That was too easy," he said, unsatisfied.

"Tell Jesus that," I said firmly.

"Jesus," Josh said, "That was too easy."

Then in the depths of Josh's heart—from his place on the

Radical Release

Cross—Jesus replied. He was stern and sober and his words bore down with the gravity of all the sins he bore on Good Friday, "NO, Josh. No. It. Wasn't."

EASY IS NOT EASY

Forgiveness is NOT easy. The Passion—the torture and death, the burden of our sin—cost Christ everything. Forgiveness is not easy for those who've been devastated by the hurts and trespasses (violations) of others. And forgiveness is not easy for those who've long condemned themselves as unforgivable.

It's hard for me to write about forgiveness through my own backstory. I cannot speak of forgiveness lightly in view of the great harm done by David or Josh or me or you. Seated on both sides of the terrible table of offense, whether fantasizing vengeance for the victims or empathizing with the offenders, forgiveness is the most demanding, excruciating process we'll ever experience.

Forgiveness is cruciformity itself.

So, whatever it was, the Cross of forgiveness is not "easy." Least of all for Jesus Christ. We pray, "Thine is the kingdom, the power and the glory," but we might just as well pray, "Thine is the sin, the sorrow and the shame of the Cross, forever and ever. Amen."

Thanks be to God. And Lord, have mercy.

But that's my story. You have yours. I know forgiveness is hard and often truly unresolvable in this lifetime. But listen: there is NO workable plan B. UnChristlike Christianity has proven this on a grand scale. The *skandalon* of God's grace—the mercy that endures forever—is the narrow path and only

Way that doesn't dead-end in our self-inflicted hells. I can't tell you to take up such a cross; I only know Jesus told me to take up mine. Some days I do.

But it's not always so hard for willing souls. Letting go is not always a gruesome crucifixion. What if instead of fighting so hard, we saw release from our offenders, our judgments and resentments as a great relief and with great joy, left those burdens behind to walk the straight and straightforward path of love?

I watched one fellow—another victim of childhood abuse—let go completely in the space of a minute. No clinging, just freedom from a lifetime pain. He told me it was like Jesus had removed a giant dagger from deep in his heart and lifted a weight the mass of our sun off his chest. Cleansing tears and great bear hugs followed. I'm jealous of the freedom I saw in his glistening eyes and new posture!

Beautiful stories of liberation abound if you pay attention. That brings us back to the adulterous woman of John 8.

"GO AND SIN NO MORE"
John 8, Genesis 3 & The Prodigal Sons

Throughout Scripture, we see "sin" identified in a variety of ways, including moral failure, law-breaking, poor spiritual hygiene, character flaws, a fatal disease and a sinister slave-driver. And where sin (hamartia) is defined as "missing the mark," Scripture implies the mark we're aiming at may be morality, holiness, faith and faithfulness, love of God and each other, or the glory of God.

Radical Release

But ultimately, I would suggest another mark: our love union with God—or RE-union (reconciliation) with God. In that case, to "sin" is to turn away from God's love. Yes, some of those other biblically-defined marks may play into that, but let's focus on three stories:

GENESIS 2-3

In the Garden of Eden (Paradise), Adam and Eve walked in perfect communion with God. Theirs was the intended love-union we were all to enjoy. And then we read of their "fall." Although the story doesn't use the term for 'sin,' we read about how they turned from that union, marked by love and trust, to autonomy, self-will and as a result, shame and alienation. Their sin does not separate God from them, for he continues to pursue them, all the way out of the garden and ultimately tracks them through the Cross to retrieve them from the depths of hades. But their sin does alienate them from God, for their new, fallen instinct is to see God as one from whom they must hide in shame. In failing to trust and obey God, and by turning from God's face to go their own way, they missed the mark of that once-perfect love-union.

THE PRODIGAL SONS

In Christ's parable of the prodigal son(s), we find two sons in similar peril. Like Adam and Eve, the younger son has left his father's house to go his own way and do his own thing. He finds himself living in the poverty of alienation, slaving in the fields with a herd of swine. He has missed the mark of fellowship with his loving father. But the father never stopped loving him and the son never ceased to be his father's son. To be restored, he must return home and re-enter the joy of that parent-child union.

Likewise, the older son finds himself slaving in another field—the field of religious striving. While he seems to serve his father's interests and seems to obey his father's wishes, he has nevertheless missed the mark. How so? He has left the father's house and made his own alleged obedience the occasion for alienation from that love-union. He regards his father as unfair, someone to resent and the elder is every bit as enslaved to self-will as his younger brother.

But the Father despises neither son. He runs to the younger son while still a long way off. And without any condemnation, he assures the older brother of his place and pleads with him to return. Henri Nouwen, in his booklet, *The Return of the Prodigal Son*, says,

> The harsh and bitter reproaches of the [elder] son are not met with words of judgment. There is no recrimination or accusation. The father does not defend himself or even comment on the elder son's behavior. The father moves directly beyond all evaluations to stress his intimate relationship with his son when he says: "You are with me always."
>
> The father's declaration of unqualified love eliminates any possibility that the younger son is more loved than the elder. The elder son has never left the house. The father has shared everything with him. He has made him part of his daily life, keeping nothing

Radical Release

from him. "All I have is yours," he says. There could be no clearer statement of the father's unlimited love for his elder son. Thus, the father's unreserved, unlimited love is offered wholly and equally to both sons.

JOHN 8: "GO AND SIN NO MORE"

This brings us to the climax of the story of the woman who was caught in the act of committing adultery. As often as I share this story, I continue to ask, "Where was the man?" Why was he not also dragged in? Was he not involved in the sin? Or was he part of the set-up? We know from the text that the whole scenario was a trap for Jesus, so it certainly looks like a case of entrapment for the woman as well.

Let's fast-forward through Jesus' saving acts—how he stoops beside her, scribbles in the dust and one by one, all the accusers leave. We pick up on Jesus' interaction with the woman, a conversation we only know because she would have shared it 1000 times thereafter. "The day Jesus saved me!"

"Where are your accusers?"

"They're gone, m'Lord."

"Neither do I condemn you. Go and sin no more."

Religious legalism would and has inferred, "Go and sin no more ... or I will condemn you."

But aside from such silliness, how should we take Jesus' statement? If he doesn't mean, "Go, be sinless," what does he mean? He must mean something!

I have normally interpreted Jesus' words this way:

"There! I've just wiped your record clean. You didn't even

repent and I forgave you. You can live as if today had never happened. And you never need to go back there. I've given you a fresh start and a new life. What will you do with it?"

To which I imagine her reply, "I will follow you, of course! I'll follow you forever!"

He smiles and says, "Of course you will. Let me help you up."

That got me thinking: what if she did it—I mean, what if she went and sinned no more! As in never again. What? Could she or anyone live without sin? That depends on what *sin* is. That depends on what *missing the mark* means. That depends on what the mark is.

If the mark is moral perfection, unwavering trust, perfect obedience, ritual hygiene and untainted holiness, of course she would continue to sin because we all fall short of those marks. And in that sense, she would go on sinning.

But if the mark is her love-union with Christ—his embrace of unwavering love, enduring mercy and saving Grace—I suspect she never left his embrace again. I could imagine her stumbling again and again but never again hiding in shame as did Adam or slaving again as did the prodigal brothers. I could imagine Jesus' words, "Go and sin no more," being for her, not a legal demand but a creative command, similar to "Let there be light ... and there was light!"

The love of Christ was a light turned on in the Father's house and he knew she would never leave the house again. Or if somehow she found herself tripping again on her own humanity, she would forever orient herself towards God's welcome, rather than fleeing from it back into the night.

Radical Release

In other words, sure she could "screw up," but from that day on, it was entirely possible she would not "fail." She could commit particular sins, but would never return to alienation and slavery to sin. She would know radical forgiveness as Love's liberating power to set her free and keep her free.

I cannot claim this for myself. But the story reminds me of how forgiveness and redemption restore us to the true mark—our union in Christ to *Abba's* unfailing love.

THOUGHTS

1. I hope this chapter clarifies what true forgiveness is and what it is not. Have you ever felt religious pressure to "forgive" someone or something when you knew it was premature or unsafe to do so? What do you think was happening? What was "off" in the process?

2. If true forgiveness is about "letting go"—releasing offenders, debts, hurts, burdens, ourselves, etc. to the Cross—take some time to ask *Abba* if there's anything you could leave there today. Ask, "If I were to let go of this, what gift would you give me in its place?"

3. I've shared a few graphic confessions of offenses that may seem irredeemable and unforgivable. How might these stack up against the finished work of Christ? Is his blood (forgiveness unto death) sufficient even for these crimes? If the victims cannot themselves forgive in this life, could the offender nevertheless experience forgiveness from God? If the victims cannot forgive, is there yet Grace for them as well? What role might incarceration still play despite *Abba's*

IN: INCARNATION & INCLUSION

forgiveness? What role might we play as messengers and agents of *Abba's* forgiveness?

PRAYERS

Abba, forgive them, they know not what they do. And sometimes they do.

Abba, forgive me, I know not what I do. And sometimes I do.

Christ, when I was your enemy, you forgave me. You gave your life for me.

Christ, help me forgive as you forgave.

Help me forgive my enemies. Help my victims forgive me.

Help me forgive even myself.

FINIS
In Practice:
A Consummation

I HOPE BY NOW that our exploration of the Bible, hearing a number of real testimonies and seeing these confirmations by a few key theologians have provoked you to fresh thoughts about the twin facets of Christ's unique revelation and *Abba's* all-embracing love.

Historically, holding fast to one of these truths to the neglect of the other has cornered us into insular and exclusive conclaves or left us with an untethered and nebulous spirituality. But I do have a very simple pattern of practice I'd like to suggest in closing:

SHARING OUR LIVES

It all starts with relationship. Since triune, other-centered Love is the nature of Christ in whose image we were created, and since Christ's own takeaway from the whole of Scripture was, "Love God with all you have and love your neighbor as yourself," we should always begin with relationship.

This means that our encounters with the other have, as first and final agenda, embodying the love of *Abba* and seeing Christ in them. Love first. Relationship first. How? I start by hearing their stories and hearing their hearts. "Tell me about

Finis: In Practice

your life. Where are you coming from? What's important to you? Who are your people? What life do you dream of for your children? What are your thoughts on love? On faith?"

Rather than racing to pontificate about our opinions and beliefs and arguments, we listen to the point of empathy. And we learn to empathize without having to agree. It's their story, it's their life, it's their heart, it's their faith. And if having shared their story, they're willing to hear yours, you'll be on the verge of a loving relationship, which Christ showed us is the point.

SHARING OUR COMMON GROUND

As fellow humans, we share much in common with everyone. We share common dreams, fears, griefs and loves. Most of us desire peace of mind and heart and a place of belonging. But even across faiths, we share a common spiritual hunger, even with New Agers. We share a common belief in the God of Abraham with Muslims and Jews. We share a common belief in the Creator with First Nations people. And no, we don't see these beliefs in the same way—of course not. But these are the days for "blessed peacemakers" who deescalate religious hostility and sectarian violence. We'll get to the differences, but first, could we acknowledge the common ground intrinsic to Paul's generous view of *Abba's* common Grace to *all* (as in Athens)?

Identifying and discussing common ground and common grace helps us relate, which is to say, builds relationship.

IN: INCARNATION & INCLUSION

SHARING OUR DIFFERENCE

This means we hold difference respectfully. Within the common ground of relationship, we can grow into the mature space of "holding difference." What an enormous relief when we discover that *real relationships are not contingent on sameness.* Our differences don't need to divide us, because divine love transcends even our central belief systems. Indeed, diversity is the very environment where love becomes manifest. In fact, *authentic otherness is the only real proving ground for Christlike love.* It is the environment where I not only honor the unique truth-claims of the other, but I can also *be open* about my own core convictions and *remain faithful* to them ... and to Christ.

In practice, this means developing our relationships sufficiently to say, "I want to know you. As you are. While we share some common ground, I suspect there are non-negotiables in our beliefs that need not be deal-breakers in our relationship. Is there something you believe so strongly that letting it go would be turning away from truest self? Something you think I might not be able to agree with? I'd love for you to know that I respect your convictions even when I don't share them. That our relationship can handle it."

Sadly, we normally get into arguments before this point. Why is that? It may be that we've launched into our differences before we've committed to relationship. Or we may think faithfulness means defending our truth zealously and attacking whatever doesn't align with it. And it may be that

Finis: In Practice

we've mistaken evangelism for making people conform and convert to our way of thinking. How's that working for us? It's not. But if it's not that, what about sharing our faith?

SHARING OUR FAITH

Our problem is that we've often misunderstood what "evangelism" was. Instead of being witnesses to the good news, we've often slid into the role of judge and jury, defense attorney or prosecutor, or even the defensive defendant. Not. Our. Job. When evangelism sounds like an accusation or a judgment or a slippery defense, the conversation is over. But if our lives (not just our words) bear witness to good news, what we say should sound like good news. The tone will sound like an invitation to love, not in *my* faith, but within our relationship.

If we have actually walked the previous steps of sharing our lives, sharing our common ground and sharing our differences respectfully, then I imagine we've already "shared the good news."

As I see it, the good news is that Christ uniquely revealed *Abba's* love for all, including the person in front of me. The invitation is that *we* would experience the Lamb-like love of *Abba's* self-giving Grace in our friendship. The gospel embodied in our relationship allows us to experience Christ in each other and enjoy *Abba's* love together. They may not see it exactly that way, but having shared my heart, if they receive me, they receive the One who is in me. And if I receive them as if I was welcoming Christ, I will encounter Christ in them.

IN: INCARNATION & INCLUSION

As we journey together, my hope is that the love of Christ will grow clearer in me and clearer to them, so we find ourselves at last sharing a common meal at Christ's common Table.

FINAL THOUGHTS

You've read my opinion—but what's yours?

1. Are you able to hold to *Abba's* inclusive love for all? Do you see limits and conditions to his love? That's not meant to be a trick question. Divine love is not imposed or coerced. So, how might our experience of God's infinite love be affected by human resistance or defiance? How does turning from *Abba's* love impact our conceptions of God and the way of our being and our way of loving?

2. Are you able to hold to the Lamb's revelation, his singular Way to *Abba?* How does this affect your view of other faiths? Of other *people* of faith? The uniqueness of Christ's revelation, after all, is all about *Abba's* love. But what if they don't see Christ the way you do? Is there yet room for relationship? Or even fellowship? What would loving respect for the other look like for you?

3. Perhaps by now you have learned to harmonize Christ's unique revelation and *Abba's* all-inclusive love. Do you see how the cruciform *Way* of Jesus Christ enfolds both? How about in practice? Can you offer an example?

FINAL PRAYER

Abba, Christ and Grace—All-merciful triune Love—eternal Word and Way, Life and Light—one and only Lamb of God . . .

Finis: In Practice

cleanse my eyes and my heart to see you more clearly and love you more deeply. Give me your eyes and heart for the world and all who are in it, that I would see Christ in all and embody good news to all. Much love, precious Friend.

RESPONSE /
Jamie & Donna Winship

JAMIE AND DONNA WINSHIP *are co-founders of* Identity Exchange (www.identityexchange.com), *a training and consulting company that encourages community transformation by teaching people how to live fearlessly in their true identity.*

For twenty-five years, they served in Indonesia, Iraq, Jordan and Jerusalem, pursuing a faith that works in the real world, even where there is war and terrorism, death and conflict. They learned that the heart of Christ is to meet people on their journey—just as they are, wherever they are—as Jesus leads them on the straight path into the Kingdom of God.

They discovered and nurtured growing movements of Muslim followers of Jesus. They are Kingdom peacemakers on the Jesus Way of nonviolent transformation and Abba's radical mercy.

KINGDOM CIRCLES

Jamie: Here is the message of the gospels, according to Jesus:

The time has come, the kingdom is at hand, repent. Change the way you think about everything and believe the new thing, which is: there is a way to live in the kingdom of God, starting now and into eternity. This is the good news. The question is, how does a person get into the kingdom of God. The way into the kingdom is through Jesus.

Response: Jamie & Donna Winship

Here's the problem: that's not what we tell people. We're all born into different sizes and shapes and ethnic groups and genders—all varieties of people, all over the world. In those different identities, we're often told or often raised to think that my identity or my group is the best, right group. And so when we meet another person from another background or another group, the message to them is if you want to live in the kingdom, you have to be like me—you have to leave your group and come into my group in order to come into the kingdom.

That message does one thing in the world. It produces conflict. This isn't really the "straight way" in that Jesus talks about. Here is the reality of what Jesus is saying: you can be who you are and walk in your own identity, through Jesus, straight into the kingdom. That's the amazing thing. And although there is only one way to the Father—through Jesus—Jesus is on every road and he is welcoming us into the Kingdom through him and not by trying to be something we're not. That way, the kingdom of God is not all just people like me, who think the way I think, but it's this diverse, beautiful "all nations of every tongue and tribe and ethnic group," joining in the kingdom of God and transformed in unity and diversity, thanking God and praising God.

IN CONVERSATION

Brad: What does Jesus mean by, "I am the Way?" If I hear you right, it's at least this: whatever and wherever our respective journeys, Jesus will meet us there and lead us on a straight path into the Kingdom of God. Indeed, he is the Shepherd, the

Path, the Door to knowing and experiencing God as all-merciful Love.

In short, Jesus is the straight path from wherever we are into the Kingdom of God.

Jamie: Bingo! We ask the questions, to what and to where is Jesus the Way? Jesus is the Way to everywhere and everything that is "kingdom." To which truth is Jesus pointing us? All truth. To what life is Jesus the source and access? All life. And Jesus is in every road.

Brad: "Jesus is in every road." Wow! And why? One answer: because he has united himself with every traveler and embedded himself in their journey. To adjust the old hymn, "Just where I am."

Jamie: Yes. Since all things are held together within Christ the Master Reconciler, who is reconciling all things to God, we would be hard-pressed to find a road he isn't on. Yes, embedded within the journey itself. I like that idea.

Brad: Thinking about articulation: it may help to distinguish "path" and "journey," where journey refers to the traveler on a path (the person on their way) while paths signify particular ways or traditions.

Jesus plants hints and signposts on those paths, even though the paths may meander and may take a traveler further from the kingdom of God. But since the journey refers to each person's life story, and since Christ is forever walking with us, he is found in every journey all the time, even on those paths that formally oppose him.

For example, the path of atheism rejects Christ, yet there he

Response: Jamie & Donna Winship

is! Accompanying atheists on their journey, Muslims on their journey, Christians on their journey, continually inviting us to follow him onto his straight path into the Kingdom of God (the reign of perfect love, joy, peace, hope and freedom in our lives).

Jamie: Fantastic!

Brad: So, we're in sync?

Jamie: Very much so.

ON THE GROUND
"FATIMA"

Donna: Jamie and I were living in the Middle East and we had a good friend there who we had met in another country—I'll call her Fatima. Her country was very war-torn. We knew her family and her father asked us if we could watch over her where we lived so she could live in safety. As a single woman, it wasn't appropriate for her to live without the protection of a family, so to be able to protect her was a very great honor for us. She lived together with some of the other single girls on our team who we were training and who were in our care.

We were training them in how to learn what the Qur'an has to say about Jesus through a study we had developed called "The Seven Signs." The course goes through seven prophets of the Old Testament that Muslims and Christians have in common, leading to Jesus as the ultimate Sign of God and ultimate sacrifice so that they could understand what it means that Jesus is the Messiah.

We had explained the "Kingdom Circles" [above] with her.

IN: INCARNATION & INCLUSION

Now she was somewhat interested in learning about the Kingdom of God and how both Muslims and Christians can follow the Straight Path into the Kingdom and live as brothers and sisters. We asked if she'd be interested in doing a Holy Book study (our Seven Signs course). She agreed, partly because she was curious but also out of respect because I was an older woman and because her good friend was also inviting her. She wanted to show honor to her friend and me.

So, we started the study and in the beginning, she was a bit bored and was going through the motions. We went through the first prophets—Adam, Abraham and Moses—but then we got to the Sign of David. In the Qur'an, the Sign of David is the Psalms, exemplified through King David. I asked her, "Is it okay if I read a Psalm to you?"

I asked because her culture and tradition says the Bible is corrupt. The Qur'an doesn't actually say that, but her culture and her tradition do, so Muslims typically don't want to have anything to do with the Bible. But when I asked her if I could read a Psalm to her, she agreed, so I chose Psalm 139.

It begins,

[1] O Lord, You have searched me and known me.
[2] You know my sitting down and my rising up;
You understand my thought afar off.
[3] You comprehend my path and my lying down,
And are acquainted with all my ways.
[4] For there is not a word on my tongue,
But behold, O Lord, You know it altogether.

Response: Jamie & Donna Winship

> ⁵ You have hedged me behind and before,
> And laid Your hand upon me.
> ⁶ Such knowledge is too wonderful for me;
> It is high, I cannot attain it...

As I'm reading through it, Fatima tears up and gets very emotional. She says, "I had no idea that the Bible sounds so much like the Qur'an. I thought it was a corrupt book, full of pornography and murder. I had no idea it was so poetic and sounds like the Qur'an!"

That night, she asked her friend if she could borrow her Bible—she wanted to be able to read the Bible for herself.

The study went on three or four more weeks until we get to the final lesson on Jesus. Our little team is praying about how to introduce Fatima to Jesus. We had another woman with us who was already a Muslim follower of Christ and she was super excited because she was good friends with Fatima.

It occurred to us that after we studied the Sign of Jesus, we could talk about the Samaritan woman. We felt that our friend Fatima was, in her true identity, a leader. And we wanted her to see how the Samaritan woman, in her true and Jesus-redeemed identity, became a leader of men—a leader in her city.

Beforehand, we had sensed in the Spirit that we should have some glasses of water out for everybody—Fatima didn't know what they were for.

We went through the story and at the end of the story, we said, "Let's just listen to what Allah wants us to know about this," because Fatima was still struggling to understand the importance of Jesus. But she loved the Samaritan woman part.

We closed our eyes and prayed, "Allah, what do you want Fatima to know about Jesus?"

She got emotional and opened her eyes and said, "I see a man and he's standing there with a book. And I'm standing with my friend [the young gal on our team] before him."

I asked her, "Who's the man?"

She said, "Well, of course it's Mohammed, peace be upon him!"

I asked, "What's the book?"

And she said, "The Qur'an, of course!"

I was a little flabbergasted and everyone on the team started looking at each other, thinking, "Hmm, this isn't going how we thought it would go." Then suddenly, this flash of inspiration came, "Don't ask her who that person is or what the book is. Have Fatima ask *Me* who the person is."

So we said, "Wait a minute. Let's ask Allah about the person who is holding the book." And we prayed, "Allah, what do you want Fatima to know about this person and this book?"

She listened for a moment and started weeping. Then she opened her eyes and said, "Allah says it's Jesus. And the book he's holding is the Book of Life. And Jesus wrote our names in the Book of Life in blood with his finger!"

Then she saw the glasses of water and said, "I want this living water. I want to drink this living water."

Then even our other Muslim friend who is a follower of Jesus said, "I already believe all of this and I want to drink the water again too!"

Response: Jamie & Donna Winship

And so, with that drink of water, she took her first communion experience.

Jamie: Fatima went home and told her father. We have this rule that whatever a young Muslim learns from us, they need to tell their parents immediately so there is no secrecy or subversiveness because Satan loves rumor. So she went and called her dad and told him what had happened. He said he wanted to meet me after that. When I went and met with him, he said, "I am so grateful because my daughter has never been this spiritual and I've always wanted her to be. By the way, I have another daughter that needs a place to live, so . . .

APPENDIX I
Five Witnesses: A Confirmation

"I PRAY THEE, O MERCIFUL LORD, for *all* the peoples of the world, that they may come to know Thee by the Holy Spirit."
—St. Silouan the Athonite

FAITHFULNESS

I want to believe that *Abba's* love could be this good—that he's "allowed" to hear the prayers of *all* who seek the Light. That he sees the hungry faith of those who've not yet heard the Name of the Lamb, and that he may even "reckon them as righteous." I want to believe that those most enslaved to sin and most shattered by sin are never beyond *Abba's* love and care. Do you?

If you're still worried that Christ's revelation of *Abba's* radical inclusion is too "out there," or that the beautiful gospel sounds too good to be true, why might that be?

Among those who hope in the wideness of God's mercy, I know some hesitate only because of their deep desire to be faithful. They would rather hold fast to the truth of Christ than exchange it for a false gospel that tickles the ears.

Me too! Whether inherited or developed, I love this truly

Appendix: Five Witnesses

conservative impulse, for it seeks to *conserve* "the faith once delivered." I share that desire. It's why I began this study with the uniqueness of Jesus Christ. It's also why I listen closely to the three-fold witness of (i) the Bible, (ii) the historic Christian faith and (iii) real-life testimonies.

Through these voices, I learned *Abba's* love is infinitely higher, wider, deeper and longer than I had dared imagine. Instead of leading me to the teetering limbs of post-Christian ideology, I traced my way down deep to our primitive Christian roots. What, or rather *Who* I discovered there surprised me. This **Word**, this **Light** was far more radical than today's bland and barren truthless spirituality. This **Lamb**, this **Christ** is far more beautiful and inviting than every brittle, narrow fundamentalism.

Here was a Treasury of substantive faith, offering me a life "anchored with wings" (h/t Peter Fitch). I found Christ and his gospel again for the first time.

So, if the challenge truly is faithfulness, rather than simply fear of seeing beyond our religious constructs and ghettos, I'm confident that we're onto something.

All that to say, I'll leave you with the testimonies of four key saints and one modern catechist of stature who I've come to trust as faithful witnesses. They assure me that when it comes to *Abba's* boundless love, we've not even begun to scratch the surface. Their vision takes my breath away, which I take as a clue to the presence of the eternal Spirit who inspired them.

IN: INCARNATION & INCLUSION

FAITHFUL WITNESSES

St. Justin Martyr (2nd century)
Apologist

Christ is the firstborn of God, his ***Logos*** (**Word**), in whom *all people* share ... *All* who have lived in accordance with the *Logos* are Christians, even if they have been reckoned atheists, as among the Greeks, Socrates, Heraclitus and the like.

—*Apology*, 1.46

St. Irenaeus of Lyons (2nd century)
Father of systematic theology

There is only one and the same God the Father, and his **Word** has been present to humanity from *all* time, although by diverse dispositions and manifold operations he has from the beginning been saving those who are saved, that is, those who love God and follow his **Word**, each in his own age.

—*Against Heresies*, 4.28.2)

St. Clement of Alexandria (150-215 A.D.)
Head of Alexandria's catechetical school

All men are Christ's, some by knowing him, the rest not yet. ... He is the Savior, *not* of some [only] and the rest not, for how is he Savior and Lord, if not the Savior and Lord of *all*? ... But he is indeed Savior of those who believe ... while of those who do not believe, he is Lord, until having become able to confess him, they obtain through him the benefit appropriate and suitable [to them]. He, by the Father's will, directs the salvation

of *all*. For *all* things have been ordered, both universally and in part, by the Lord of the universe.
—*Stromata* 7 (cited in Thomas Allin, *Christ Triumphant*, Wipf & Stock, 2015, 110).

The universe has become ceaseless light. The Sun of righteousness who traverses the universe, pervades *all* humanity alike. Giving us the alienable inheritance of the Father. . . . Writing his laws on our hearts. What laws are those he thus writes? That *all* shall know God from small to great. It is always the purpose of God to save the human flock.
—*Exhortation to the Heathen* (Ibid. 110).

St. Gregory of Nyssa (335-390 A.D.)
Final editor of the Nicene Creed

For it is evident that God will in truth be *all in all* when there shall be no evil in existence, when every created being is at harmony with itself and every tongue shall confess that Jesus Christ is Lord; when every creature shall have been made one body.
—*In illud: Tunc et Ipse Filus,* (Ibid. 131).

Olivier Clement (20th century)
Theologian and catechist, St. Sergius, Paris

For the early church, salvation is not at all reserved to the baptized. We repeat: those who receive baptism undertake to work for the salvation of *all*. The **Word** has never ceased and never will cease to be present to humanity in *all* cultures, *all*

IN: INCARNATION & INCLUSION

religions, and *all* irreligious. The incarnation and the resurrection are not exclusive but inclusive of the manifold forms of this presence...

It is certainly for Christians to make people understand that Christ comes for *all*, since he combines the maximum of humanity with the maximum of divinity. But when they fail in this, Christ himself appears to those who are dying...

Does the matter stand otherwise today for unbelievers? Christ is close to them and they are often following him without realizing it, practicing justice and kindness towards their neighbors, gaining a foretaste of the mystery through love and beauty. Christ reveals himself fully to them at the moment of their death, flooding them with sweetness and splendor. Doubtless, he has to wait about through years of hardening and spiritual insensitivity before he can rediscover the vulnerable and astonished child.

—Olivier Clement, *The Roots of Christian Mysticism* (New City Press, 2017), 296-8.

The most fundamental Trinitarian experience is inscribed in the second word of the Our Father: "Father of us."

Concerning this "us," I would like to make two points.

The first is that we must learn to discern the mystery of God in the face of our neighbor... we must understand that, whoever they may be—publicans, prostitutes or Samaritans, as Jesus says—*all* people are the image of God, children of the Father...

The other point... inseparable from the first, is the relationship between the Church and mankind: "Father of us." Is this

Appendix: Five Witnesses

"us" just the Church where we are all members of one another: a single body, one being in Christ, with each of us encountering Jesus personally, each of us being in bloom and by the one pentecostal flame? The **Word**, as the prologue of John says, "is the true **light** that enlightens *every* man who comes into the world." This has also been translated as: "... that, coming into the world, enlightens every man." In becoming incarnate, the **Word** assumed all of humanity, *every* person from every time and place. In his resurrection, he raised *all* mankind.

Whether they are many or few, the Church is comprised of those who discover all this, who lucidly enter into this **light** and give thanks on behalf of *all*. The Church is the "royal priesthood," the "holy nation" set apart to pray, to bear witness and to work for the salvation of *all* mankind. We know where the heart of the Church is: it is in the Gospel and in the Eucharist. And yet we remain unaware of the extent to which it enlightens because the Eucharist is offered "for the life of the world."

There is not one blade of grass that does not grow within the Church, not one constellation that does not revolve around the tree of the Cross, the new Tree of Life and the world's axis. There is not one person who does not have a mysterious relationship with the Father who created him, with the Son, the "ultimate man," and with this Breath that moves all living things. There is not one person who does not aspire to goodness, who does not tremble before beauty, nor is there one who is devoid of a sense of mystery when faced with love and with death.

IN: INCARNATION & INCLUSION

On the day of judgment, as they are filled with joy, many will say: "Lord, when did we see you hungry and give you food ... a stranger and welcome you, naked and clothe you? When did we see you in prison or sick and visit you? And they will hear it said to them: "Truly, I say to you, as you did it to the least of these little ones, my brothers, you did it to me!" Are we doing these things?

Let us not, in our daily lives, turn the church into a sect or a ghetto. Let us learn to discern the seeds of life in all things. Let us learn to welcome them into our understanding and our love and to gather them into our prayer within the church.

—Olivier Clement, *Three Prayers: Our Father, O Heavenly King, Prayer of St Ephrem* (St. Vladimir's Seminary Press, 2010), 10-12.

APPENDIX II
Important Definitions:
Inclusion, Pluralism, Syncretism

TAKE CARE

CRITICS MAY DISAGREE with where I come out but please be warned: it would be libelous to ignore my fervent belief in Christ's unique revelation of *Abba* and misrepresent my position as "pluralism" or "syncretism." To avoid confusion, here are a few extremely important definitions that clarify *my use* of key terms in this book. These words may have multiple meanings, so if you want to understand me, you'll need to hear what I mean when I refer to the following:

INCLUSION

When I speak of *inclusion*, I first mean Christ's inclusion of all humanity in the *hypostatic union*. That is, when the Word became flesh, Jesus Christ united himself to the entire human race. The union of divine and human natures in the one Person means that what Christ did, he did for all—his life, death, resurrection and ascension include *everyone* in the life of the Trinity.

This Good News carries with it an invitation to willingly participate in the eternal life and love of Father, Son and Spirit

Important Definitions

(perichoresis) so that the truth of our being would also become the way of our being (cf. T. F. Torrance and C. Baxter Kruger's "Trinitarian" theology).

Trinitarian inclusion is *not* necessarily universalism. Though some Trinitarians are universalists, *I am not.* But my *inclusivism* means that I hope, pray and preach that *all* will ultimately see and respond to the revelation of Christ in them (Gal. 1:16, 2 Cor. 4:40) as they discover they have already been forgiven and reconciled to *Abba* through the work of Christ (Rom. 5:6-10, Col. 1:19-20).

Second, *for me*, our inclusion into the life of the Trinity must also become manifest through the full and practical inclusion of diverse people at Christ's Open Table.

Who is welcome? Who belongs? Who is included? *ALL* who were in Adam, *all* for whom Christ came, *all* whom Christ has invited, *all* for whom Christ died. A table too small for the least and the lost, "the publican and the sinner," is not the Table of our Lord.

PLURALISM

In this book, I use "pluralism" in a theological sense that I resist. There is also a social sense that I embrace but will not be using.

The *social pluralism* I *affirm* says that in our culture and in the public world of our governments and universities, people of all faiths or no faith should have the right to express their convictions freely and have their voices heard. Social pluralism resists *secularism*, which seeks to silence faith in the public square and make society a values-free and faith-free zone.

IN: INCARNATION & INCLUSION

Secularism only tolerates a faith that remains private and out of sight. Of course, that means secularism demands that its ideology is the only and exclusive voice at the table.

But there is also a *religious pluralism that I resist* in this book. By my definition, religious pluralism sees all religions as equally valid paths and expressions of faith—that beneath the surface, they are all ultimately the same and all lead to the same God. I don't believe that.

I am not a religious pluralist. But neither am I a religious exclusivist, as if Christianity were the only hill on which the Light of God might shine. In *Abba's* generosity, a *common grace* blows where she wills and has imparted profound truth and wisdom to seekers across diverse faiths.

I believe this common Grace is the Person and work of the Holy Spirit. I believe that Jesus Christ is the fulfillment of what all faiths are ultimately seeking, and that their intimations of the Divine come to rest in our *Abba*. They may not agree with me, but apparently, God doesn't seem to wait for my stamp of approval. Common Grace means there will also be common ground for interfaith discussion, and in that respectful space, I feel free to bear witness to my convictions about the uniqueness of Jesus Christ.

SYNCRETISM

The Cambridge Dictionary defines *syncretism* as "the combining of different religions, cultures, or ideas." When it comes to religion, *I am not a syncretist.*

While various religions share a lot of common ground,

Important Definitions

mutual respect requires that we also acknowledge how each faith has a set of core dogmas, unique and exclusive to itself, and without which that faith is compromised. A syncretism that tries to combine religions will compromise the integrity of those core convictions. That's one reason why *I reject syncretism as such.*

That said, we must also think through what syncretism is *not.* Common faith practices, such as praying, singing hymns, lighting candles and meditative breathing are *not* syncretism. These are among the many humanly inspired methods of spiritual devotion, helpful ways of orienting ourselves toward the Divine. Many such practices cross traditions because they reflect our common humanity as diverse children of *Abba.*

A certain amount of borrowing also happens—we know for sure this occurred within Judaism as it adopted and adapted elements of Babylonian and Greek thought and practice through cultural engagement, even within the Bible. Sometimes the borrowing led to idolatry, while at other times it was revelatory. The Pharisees' belief in the resurrection of the dead is a profound example (Acts 23:8). Their Sadducee rivals would have accused them of syncretism.

The Jews, of necessity, experienced a profound religious evolution, but their transformation was only condemned when new practices (i) redirected worship from YAHWEH to other gods (e.g. Baal) or (ii) were intrinsically destructive and unjust (e.g. child sacrifice). These biblical criteria draw the red line between common interfaith practices and syncretism proper, where the latter is condemned as infidelity.

IN: INCARNATION & INCLUSION

WHERE CHRIST "SHOWS UP"

What's confusing today is how to interpret the reality of Christ (the Light/the Word/the Lamb) "showing up" in an alternative faith space or practice. Some balk and claim he never does. They obviously haven't wandered beyond their Christian ghetto. It happens all the time—Christ seeks and finds open hearts so that they will seek and find him, from twelve-step meetings in my own town to the night-visions of Muslims across the Middle East.

What is Christ up to? Is he affirming other faiths? Is he endorsing other practices? Is Grace accommodating to our ways or calling us from them?

Anyway, it's a strange demon that would direct one's heart to Christ and encourage surrender to the love of *Abba*.

No, not an unclean spirit at all but the Holy Spirit, serving as Christ's Forerunner Evangelist, just as he promised:

> When the advocate comes, *whom I shall send to you from the Father,* the Spirit of truth who comes forth from the Father, *he will testify concerning me;* and you too must testify, for you are with me from the beginning.
> — John 15:26-27

Of this I am certain: wherever Christ appears, even in our darkest abyss or humanity's most perverse pigpens, his ministry is reconciliation. Christ is all about seeking lost sheep wherever they've wandered, drawing *all* people to himself and beckoning us to follow him to his *Abba's* house.

Books by Bradley Jersak

More Christlike Series

A More Christlike God: A More Beautiful Gospel (CWRpress 2016).

A More Christlike Way: A More Beautiful Faith (CWRpress 2019).

A More Christlike Word (Whitaker House 2020).

Theological Works

Stricken by God? Nonviolent Atonement and the Victory of Christ (Eerdmans 2007), editor.

Her Gates Will Never Be Shut: Hope, Hell and the New Jerusalem (Wipf & Stock 2009).

From the Cave to the Cross: The Cruciform Theology of George P. Grant and Simone Weil (St Macrina 2015).

Simone Weil, *Awaiting God: A New Translation of Attente de Dieu and Lettre a Un Religieux* (Fresh Wind 2012), translator.

Clarion Call to Love: Essays in Gratitude to Archbishop Lazar Puhalo (St Macrina 2018), editor.

Children's Books

Children, Can You Hear Me? Illust. by Ken Save (Fresh Wind 2004).

Jesus Showed Us Illustrated by Shari-Ann Vis (St Macrina 2017).

Fresh Wind Press

Can You Hear Me? Tuning in to the God Who Speaks (2003).

Rivers from Eden with Eden Jersak (2004).

Kissing the Leper: Seeing Jesus in the Least of These (2006).

Political Philosophy

George P. Grant: Minerva's Snowy Owl (2014).

George P: Grant: Canada's Lone Wolf, with Ron S. Dart (2013).

Red Tory, Red Virgin: Essays on Simone Weil & George P. Grant (2013).

George Grant: Athena's Aviary, with Ron S. Dart (St Macrina 2019).

Chapter Title

Made in the USA
Columbia, SC
15 October 2020